Dear Wit

Letters from the World's Wits

H. JACK LANG

Prentice Hall

New York London Toronto Sydney Tokyo Singapore

The Acknowledgments beginning on page 260 form an integral part of this copyright notice.

First Edition

Copyright © 1990 by H. Jack Lang

Prentice Hall

Simon & Schuster, Inc.
15 Columbus Circle
New York, NY 10023

DISTRIBUTED BY PRENTICE HALL TRADE SALES

Text Design by Peter Katucki

Manufactured in the United States of America

1 2 3 4 5 6 7 8 9 10

Library of Congress Cataloging-in-Publication Data

Lang, H. Jack, 1904–
    Dear Wit : letters from the world's wits / H. Jack Lang.—1st ed.
      p.   cm.
    ISBN 0-13-961715-9
    1. Letters—Humor.   2. Wit and humor.   I. Title.
    PN6131.L36   1990   89-49534
    808.86—dc20   CIP

Contents

For Frances to whom I have dedicated
my life, including this book.

Introduction

"Wit sets a snare, whereas humor goes off whistling without a victim in its mind." So said Charles S. Brooks of one kind of wit. But wit also connotes the cleverness of a phrase that pleases rather than victimizes. Such wit implies wisdom, from the original derivation of the word, *witan*.

In this book are both kinds of wit, written in letter form, rather than spoken. This epistolary wit is categorized into *biting wit*, with its irony and sarcasm. Closely akin are *critical wit* and *boomerang wit*, where the bitten bite back. Then there is *gentle wit*, clever but without ire or insult, and the imaginative fantasies of *whimsical wit*. *Literary* and *poetic wit* recount the memorable *bon mots* of authors and poets, followed by the many witticisms of publishers, editors historical men of note, playwrights, actors, musicians, clergymen, doctors, tradesmen, and the legal-minded. Finally, there is the *wit that is wisdom*—the sage estimations of the keen-witted.

The selections necessarily reflect the anthologist's prejudices. Samuel Johnson, Mark Twain, and George Bernard Shaw are favored for their biting wit; Winston Churchill and Cornelius Otis Skinner for their rapier-like ripostes. None is more whimsical than Robert Louis Stevenson and Lewis Carroll, nor more gentle in their wit than Charles Lamb or John Steinbeck. Voltaire, Thackeray, Oscar Wilde, and Yuan Mei stand out among literary and poetic wits, while the Reverend Sydney Smith is among the most revered for the wisdom of his wit.

Rhetoricians advise that the way to learn to write well is to read the best authors. As Virginia Woolf has said, "we can read such books . . . not to throw light on literature, not to become familiar with famous people, but to refresh and exercise our own creative powers." By reading these masters of the epistolary art, we might make our own writing more witty.

This is a book that has been more than fifty years in the making. All but a few of the letters have been carefully chosen from many hundreds published, under my editorship, for half a century in *The Wolf Magazine of Letters*—a vast source, unmatched anywhere for uniqueness, cleverness, and wit.

When the magazine reached the twenty-five-year mark, I received a congratulatory letter from one of the founders of the Book of the Month Club. It read in part,

> Letters are the funniest, most tragic, most welcomed, or most feared communications of man. In them are poured the bared hearts and souls of people in all walks of life. More clearly than their apparel, their faces, or other actions, their letters tell what they are and who they are.
>
> And, among letters, as among people, only a few are worth meeting. But these few are the everlasting gems that will wear and sparkle for all time.
>
> You've done your share to unearth and preserve many of the best of the best. Keep on keeping on!

That was thirty years ago. Now, at the age of eighty-five, I still will "keep on keeping on" in the considered belief that wit and humor are the best antidotes for that melancholy mood, Weltschmerz.

H. Jack Lang

I

Biting Wit

Robert G. Ingersoll
John Ruskin
Mark Twain
Henry James
Will Rogers
George Bernard Shaw
Michael Noble, M.P.
Ilka Chase
Bertrand Russell
Alan Littman
Groucho Marx
Pablo Picasso
Adlai Stevenson
Johnny Unitas

As long as there are postmen life will have zest.
—Henry James

Robert G. Ingersoll

Colonel Robert Ingersoll frequently drew the ire of the press for his agnostic writings and speeches. When one paper alluded to Ingersoll's son as a reader of trashy novels and an insane youth who died in an asylum, the sharp-witted Colonel addressed the editor as follows:

Dear Sir:

My son was not a great novel reader. He did not go insane. He was not sent to an asylum. He did not die. I never had a son.

Robert Ingersoll

John Ruskin

John Ruskin's art criticism included an element of "petulance (amounting occasionally to rudeness)." After Ruskin condemned an artist-friend's work, he expressed the hope it would not interfere with their friendship. The offended artist responded:

Ruskin—

Next time I meet you I shall knock you down, but I hope it will make no difference in our friendship.

Unnamed Artist

Mark Twain

Librarian Asa Don Dickinson informed Mark Twain (Samuel L. Clemens) that a prudish young woman had removed *Tom Sawyer* and the author's favorite *Huckleberry Finn* from the children's department, much to Dickinson's chagrin. Twain replied with his own special blend of sarcasm and humor:

November 21, 1905

Dear Sir:

I am greatly troubled by what you say. I wrote *Tom Sawyer* and *Huck Finn* for adults exclusively, and it always distresses me when I find that boys and girls have been allowed access to them. The mind that becomes soiled in youth can never again be washed clean; I know this by my own experience, and to this day I cherish an unappeasable bitterness against the unfaithful guardians of my young life, who not only permitted but compelled me, to read an unexpurgated Bible through before I was fifteen years old. None can do that and ever draw a clean sweet breath again this side of the grave. Ask that young lady—she will tell you so.

Most honestly do I wish I could say a softening word or two in defense of Huck's character, since you wish it, but really in my opinion it is no better than those of Solomon, David, Satan, and the rest of the sacred brotherhood.

If there is an unexpurgated Bible in the children's department, won't you please help that young woman remove Huck and Tom from that questionable companionship?

Sincerely yours,

S. L. *Clemens.*

Editor's Note: *Tom Sawyer* and *Huckleberry Finn* were listed as two of the ten best books for children by The Children's Literature Association.

Henry James

In England, men who inherit their fortunes rank higher socially than men who earn theirs. A wealthy neighbor of Henry James, sensitive of his success in the jam and jelly business, rudely complained of the novelist's servants cutting the corner of his estate. Henry James sent this cutting reply:

My dear Sir:

I am deeply grieved to learn that certain of my employees have been invading your preserves. I assure you the offense shall not be repeated.

Yours respectfully,

Henry James

P.S. I beg your pardon for using the word "preserves."

Will Rogers

Playing in the Ziegfeld Follies during World War I, Will Rogers received a heckling letter from a young woman asking, "Why aren't you in the army?" Rogers replied:

For the same reason, Madam, that you aren't in the Follies—physical disabilities.

Will Rogers

George Bernard Shaw

George Bernard Shaw was known for his curt, Shavian wit, as expressed in this exchange between Winston Churchill's mother and the irrepressible G. B. S.:

Mr. George Bernard Shaw:

Lady Randolph Churchill will be home on Thursday afternoon, next, at four o'clock, RSVP.

To which the candid sage replied:

So will George Bernard Shaw.

Michael Noble, M.P.

Living up to the centuries' old British tradition of courtesy, a canny member of Parliament sent this note to the letters column of the Campbeltown, Scotland; *Courier*:

Dear Sirs:

Mr. Michael Noble, Argyllshire's M.P. . . . will be replying to Mr. Denis McKay (*Courier*, December 18) after the season of good will is over.

M.N.

Ilka Chase

Actress Ilka Chase's marriage to actor Louis Calhern lasted only six months. When he remarried, Ilka sent the second Mrs. Calhern a box of unused calling cards, engraved, "Mrs. Louis Calhern," with this note:

Dear Julia:

Hope these reach you in time.

Ilka

Bertrand Russell

When a professor at Western Reserve University wrote asking Bertrand Russell to fill out a long and personal questionnaire, the fiery old sage sent this reply:

Dear Sir,

If this is a specimen of Western reserve, God protect me from Western impudence.

Bertrand Russell

Alan Littman

While visiting London, Alan Littman, former president of The Wolf Envelope Company, noticed a baby carriage parked outside a shop, with this note pinned on it:

WARNING: Do not bend over to pet or coo over this child. Although born in wedlock he is a little bastard.

His Mother

Groucho Marx

Groucho Marx was renowned for his bizarre wisecracks. As Leo Rosten put it, "Groucho Marx perfected the logic of lunacy." When invited to become a member of a club, he replied:

Dear Sir,

I do not wish to belong to the kind of club that accepts people like me as members.

Groucho Marx

Pablo Picasso

Rene Gimpel, in his *Diary of an Art Dealer*, wrote that a lady once wrote Pablo Picasso asking for an appointment to have her portrait painted. The great but temperamental artist sent this reply:

Madam,

> You need only send me a lock of hair and your necklace.

> *Picasso*

Adlai Stevenson

There is the story, as told by Bill Adler in *The Stevenson Wit*, about the congressman who wrote to Adlai complaining that the stationery watermarked with the Illinois state seal was being used by a gambler to offer tips on races. Stevenson, then governor of Illinois, sent this reply:

Dear Sir:

> Your taste for unverified accusations reminds me of the lawyer who said to the jury: "These are the conclusions on which I base my facts."

> *Adlai Stevenson*

Johnny Unitas

Hospitalized with a torn Achilles tendon, Don Rickles, who makes a living out of being unpleasant, received this terse message from gridiron great Johnny Unitas:

Don Rickles,

It couldn't have happened to a nicer heel.

Johnny Unitas

I I

Boomerang Wit

Alexandre Dumas *père*
Cornelius Vanderbilt and George Westinghouse
James McNeill Whistler and Oscar Wilde
Sir James M. Barrie and A. E. Housman
Dorothy Thompson
Sari Maritza
Alexander Woollcott and Bennett Cerf
George Bernard Shaw and Winston Churchill
George Bernard Shaw and Cornelia Otis Skinner
Charlie Feldman and Sir Alexander Korda
Leo Rosten
Jack Benny and Ace Goodman

The wit makes fun of other persons; the satirist makes fun of the world; the humorist makes fun of himself.

—*James Thurber*

Alexandre Dumas *père*

When a young, would-be author wrote to Alexandre Dumas *père* suggesting they collaborate in writing a novel, the widely-read author of *The Three Musketeers* sharply answered:

Dear Sir,

How dare you, sir, yoke together a noble horse and a contemptible ass?

Alexandre Dumas

The young man replied:

Dear Mr. Dumas:

How dare you, sir, call me a horse?

S. S.

Amused and no longer angered, Dumas wrote back:

Dear Sir:

Send me your manuscript, my friend; I gladly accept your proposition.

A. D.

Cornelius Vanderbilt
and George Westinghouse

In 1872, when George Westinghouse asked Cornelius Vanderbilt to listen to his idea for inventing an air brake, the crusty president of the New York Central replied:

I have no time to waste on fools.

Vanderbilt

After the Pennsylvania Railroad successfully tested it, Vanderbilt invited Westinghouse to see him. The inventor replied:

I have no time to waste on fools.

Westinghouse

James McNeill Whistler
and Oscar Wilde

A gossip column in an English newspaper once reported: "James McNeill Whistler and Oscar Wilde were seen yesterday, talking as usual about themselves." Whistler sent the column to Wilde with this note:

Dear Wilde:

I wish these reporters would be accurate. If you remember, Oscar, we were talking about me.

Whistler

Never one to be outdone, Wilde replied:

Dear Whistler:

It is true, Jimmie, we were talking about you, but I was thinking of myself!

Wilde

Sir James M. Barrie
and A. E. Housman

Two shy authors, Sir James M. Barrie (*Peter Pan*) and A. E. Housman (A *Shropshire Lad*), sat next to each other at a Cambridge University dinner without exchanging a word. The next day Barrie sent this letter:

Dear Professor Houseman,

I am sorry about last night, when I sat next to you and did not say a word. You must have thought I was a very rude man; I am really a very shy man.

Sincerely yours,

J. M. *Barrie*

Professor Housman replied:

Dear Sir James Barrie,

I am sorry about last night, when I sat next to you and did not say a word. You must have thought I was a very rude man; I am really a very shy man.

Sincerely yours,

A. E. *Housman*

P.S.   And now you've made it worse for you have spelt my name wrong.

Dorothy Thompson

Sinclair Lewis was the first American to win the Nobel Prize for literature. At the peak of his popularity, a young lady applied for the position of his secretary. "Dear Mr. Lewis," she wrote, "I'll do everything for you—and when I say everything I mean everything." The reply was prompt:

My dear Miss————:

My husband already has a stenographer who handles his work for him. And, as for "everything" I take care of that myself—and when I say everything I mean everything.

Dorothy Thompson
(Mrs. Sinclair Lewis to you.)

Sari Maritza

As Maurice Chevalier told it, a movie director proposed to Sari Maritza at a Hollywood party. The next day he sent her this note:

Dear Sari,

Imagine my embarrassment! Last night I asked you to marry me. Now I can't remember whether you said yes or no.

A———

By return mail came this reply:

My dear,

Your letter brought me infinite relief. I knew that I refused last night to marry someone—but for the life of me I couldn't remember whom.

Sari

Alexander Woollcott
and Bennett Cerf

Alexander Woollcott once publicly derided Bennett Cerf's Random House for publishing what Woollcott considered an unscholarly translation of Proust. Some years later, after reading a Random House book he liked, Woollcott wrote:

Dear Cerf:

By some miracle you have published a book which is not second rate.
Please send me twelve copies at once.

Yours sincerely,

A. *Woollcott*

"Try and Stop Me" Cerf was quick to reply:

Dear Woollcott:

By some miracle you can *buy* those twelve copies at Brentano's.

Yours very truly,

Bennett Cerf

George Bernard Shaw
and Winston Churchill

The feisty, old sage G. B. S. seldom came out second best as he did in this waspish exchange with canny "Winnie" Churchill:

My dear Churchill:

Herewith are two tickets for the opening of my new play; one for you and one for a friend of yours—if any.

G. B. S.

Dear Shaw:

A previous engagement prevents my using the opening-night tickets, which I am returning herewith. I would appreciate it if you would send me tickets for the second performance—if any.

Winston Churchill

Dan H. Laurence, editor of the four volumes of Shaw's letters, indicates that this oft-quoted, clever exchange is of questionable authenticity. As proof, Laurence includes Shaw's crusty reply at the bottom of a request to publish the letters:

The above is not only a flat lie but a political libel which may possibly damage me. Publish it at your peril, whether in assertion or contradiction.

G. *Bernard Shaw*

Editor's Note: In his graphic description of G. B. S.'s last days, Dan Laurence reports that Shaw's doctor allegedly affirmed that G. B. S. told him of this correspondence with Churchill, although Laurence says that this too is probably apocryphal.

George Bernard Shaw
and Cornelia Otis Skinner

This spirited exchange of cables followed the New York opening of George Bernard Shaw's *Candida*, in which Cornelia Otis Skinner played the leading role:

Cornelia Otis Skinner
New York, USA

> Excellent! Greatest!
>
> G.B.S.

George Bernard Shaw
London, England

> Undeserving such praise.
>
> *Cornelia*

Cornelia Otis Skinner
New York, USA

> Meant the play.
>
> G.B.S.

George Bernard Shaw
London, England

> So did I.
>
> *Cornelia*

Charlie Feldman and Sir Alexander Korda

Charlie Feldman, agent-producer, liked to play gin with London Films producer Alexander Korda. Once, when Feldman lost, he mailed Korda a check written in red ink with this note:

Dear Alec:

You will see that this check is written in blood.

Charlie

In their next game, Korda lost but got the last word when he sent Feldman a check written in blue ink with this comment:

Dear Charlie:

Herewith my check. Please note it is also written in blood—but be sure to note the difference in color.

Sir Alexander Korda

Leo Rosten

Author Leo Rosten receives many crank letters from readers, but none more insulting than this:

Dear Sir,

I bet you are a dirty atheist.

Too late, Rosten thought of the answer which he wished he had sent:

Dear Sir,

You lose. I bathe at least once a day and invoke God's help with great fervor whenever I encounter someone like you.

Leo Rosten

Jack Benny and Ace Goodman

When gag writer Ace Goodman sent Jack Benny one of his best jokes, the parsimonious Benny sent him a fifty dollar check with this note:

Dear Ace,

Your joke got lots of laughs. If you have any more, send them along.

Jack

The past master of wisecracks replied:

Dear Jack,

Your check got lots of laughs. If you have any more, send them along.

Ace

III

Critical Wit

Francois Marie Arouet de Voltaire
Samuel Johnson
Benjamin Disraeli
Alphonse Daudet
Eugene Field
John Jay Chapman (William Dean Howells)
Marc Hamblot
James Whitcomb Riley
Somerset Maugham
William Lyon Phelps
George Horace Lorimer
Joseph Cornelius

Letters are valuable and entertaining in proportion to the wit and ability and above all to the imprudence, of those who write them.

—C.E. *Vulliamy*

Francois Marie Arouet de Voltaire

When Jean-Jacques Rousseau finished his "Ode to Posterity," he sent a copy to Voltaire. The ever skeptical Voltaire returned it with this single, caustic sentence:

Dear Rousseau:

> This poem will never reach its destination.

Voltaire

Samuel Johnson

"Though he was good-natured at bottom, he was very ill-natured at top." So wrote Horace Walpole of Samuel Johnson. When a young writer asked him to comment on his work, the irritable lexicographer put it bluntly:

Dear Sir:

> Your work is both good and original. But the part that is good is not original. And the part that is original is not good.

Samuel Johnson

Benjamin Disraeli

Benjamin Disraeli, favorite of Queen Victoria, was both a statesman and author. His patience was tried by would-be writers sending him crude samples of their work for his criticism. This was his usual reply:

Dear Sir,

Many thanks; I shall lose no time reading it.

Benjamin Disraeli

Alphonse Daudet

An editor once asked Alphonse Daudet to write an article of congratulations to Emile Zola upon his completing twenty volumes on the Rougon-Macquart family. This was Daudet's reply, as told by Betty Jo Ramsey in *The Little Book of Famous Insults*:

Dear Sir,

If I were to write that article, it would be to advise Zola, now that the family-tree of the Rougon-Macquarts is complete, to go and hang himself from the highest branch.

Alphonse Daudet

Eugene Field

When a would-be poet asked Eugene Field for criticism of some verse he had written entitled, "Why Do I Live?," the author of *Little Boy Blue* sent this reply:

Dear Sir:

Because you sent your poem by mail.

Eugene Field

John Jay Chapman
(William Dean Howells)

Poet John Jay Chapman quotes a bit of biting criticism offered by novelist William Dean Howells to a budding author:

On the train Thanksgiving day, 1911

Dear Daisy,

... Did you hear what Howells once said to a boring author who was trying to wring a compliment out of him? "I don't know how it is," said the author. "I don't seem to *write* as well as I used to do." "Oh, yes, you do—indeed you do [replied Howells]. You write as well as you ever did—But your *taste* is improving." ...

Yours affectionately,

Jack

Marc Hamblot

In 1912 a French editor turned down the novel *Swann's Way* by the verbose Marcel Proust with this sardonic note. Proust published the classic novel at his own expense:

Dear Mr. Proust,

My dear fellow, I may perhaps be dead from the neck up, but rack my brains as I may I can't see why a chap should need thirty pages to describe how he turns over in bed.

Marc Hamblot, Editor

James Whitcomb Riley

In his poetry, but particularly his correspondence, James Whitcomb Riley was widely known as the "Untamed Hoosier." This letter to a young lady seeking advice is one of the reasons why:

Portland, Oregon
December 25, 1892

Dear Miss,

Your poem here seems to be an unconscious echo of Tennyson's "Break, Break, Break." The comparison of the two poems, I doubt not, will startle you—in almost every line . . .

If, therefore, this is an "average specimen" of your verse, for me to "frankly judge its worth by," I would not advise you to "write for publication." Though Mr. Tennyson is dead now, he has still a belated friend or two yet in the earth-life who might wittily get back at you by removing other effects of his from your temptation.

Very truly your friend—and also Mr. Tennyson's,

James Whitcomb Riley

Somerset Maugham

These terse notes were exchanged by Somerset Maugham and a young lady who had submitted some short stories to the famous author for criticism:

Dear Mr. Maugham:

Do you think I should put forth more fire into my stories?

Ann Onymous

The noted author of *Of Human Bondage* replied:

Dear Miss Onymous:

No. Vice versa.

Somerset Maugham

William Lyon Phelps

In the freshman English class, a coed submitted a paper containing the sentence: "The lady was descending the stairs when she tripped, fell, and lay prostitute on the floor." The professor circled the offending word, and added this note. In his *Anguished English*, Richard Lederer reports that this note has been attributed to William Lyon Phelps of Yale and others:

My dear young lady,

You must learn to distinguish between a fallen woman and one who has temporarily lost her balance.

William Lyon Phelps

George Horace Lorimer

When George Horace Lorimer, famed *Post* editor, returned a rejected manuscript with pages 800 and 801 transposed, the indignant author wrote, "I transposed those pages just to prove you do not read my stories." Lorimer replied:

My dear sir:

Is it necessary to eat all of an egg to find out it is bad?

George Horace Lorimer

Joseph Cornelius

Joseph Cornelius, one-time president of the Bank of Clearwater, Florida, sent this joshing answer to a letter from a friend:

Dear Macks:

. . . Somehow I feel this letter is not as effervescent, exhilirating, exciting, exotic, ebullient, ecstatic, effusive, exultant, elating, elegant, eloquent, enriching, entertaining, enthusiastic, enticing, erudite, esoteric, or expressive as some of those sent you in the past.

I referred it to one of the English professors at the University of Tampa. He said, "Your vocabulary is mean and impoverished but entirely adequate to express your thoughts."

Hoping you are not the same,

Sincerely,

Joe

I V

Gentle Wit

Charles Lamb
Sydney Smith
Charles de Talleyrand
T. B. Aldrich
Mark Twain
H. G. Wells
Gelett Burgess
Winston Churchill
Ruth Van Bergen
Vic Gelb
Herman "Fritz" Liebert
Miss Manners

Letters make the most interesting reading in the world—especially other people's.
—M. *Lincoln Schuster*

Charles Lamb

After Charles Lamb had cavorted in an unbecoming manner at a party given by Dr. and Mrs. Asbury, he composed this good-humored apology at the insistence of his sister Mary, with whom he wrote *Tales From Shakespeare*:

April, 1830

Dear Sir:

It is an observation of a wise man that "moderation is best in all things." I cannot agree with him "in liquor." There is a smoothness and oiliness in wine that makes it go down by a natural channel, which I am positive was made for that descending. . . .

Still there is something due to manners and customs, and I should apologize to you and Mrs. Asbury for being absolutely carried home upon a man's shoulders thro' Silver Street, up Parson's Lane, by the Chapels (which might have taught me better), and then to be deposited like a dead log at Gaffar Westwood's . . .

Still you will say (or the men and maids at your house will say) that it is not a seemly sight for an old gentleman to go home pickaback. Well, maybe it is not. But I never studied grace. . . .

Here I am, able to compose a sensible, rational apology, and what signifies how I got here. I have just sense enough to remember I was very happy last night, and to thank our kind host and hostess, and that's sense enough, I hope.

Charles Lamb

Sydney Smith

The Reverend Sydney Smith was canon at St. Paul's and one of England's foremost wits. In this letter, he declined an invitation from a friend with his inevitable sense of humor:

Dear Longman,

I can't accept your invitation, for my house is full of country cousins. I wish they were once removed.

Sydney Smith

Charles de Talleyrand

The French statesman Talleyrand was one of the most laconic of letter writers. After hearing from a lady friend that she had lost her husband, Talleyrand sent this note:

My dear Comtesse,

Alas!

Your most devoted

Talleyrand

When a year or so later the same lady wrote to tell him she had remarried, the French diplomat replied:

My dear Comtesse,

Oh! Oh!

Your most devoted

Talleyrand

T. B. Aldrich

Many of our best writers have been illegible writers. Some works of Shakespeare and Hawthorne have never been deciphered. Napoleon's letters were often mistaken for battlefield maps. Thomas Bailey Aldrich acknowledged a cryptic scrawl from a friend as follows:

Dear Mr. Morse:

It was very pleasant to me to get a letter from you the other day. Perhaps I should have found it pleasanter if I had been able to decipher it. I don't think I have mastered anything beyond the date (which I knew) and the signature (which I knew).

There is a singular and perpetual charm in a letter of yours—it never grows old; it never loses its novelty. One can say to oneself every morning: "There's that letter of Morse's. I haven't read it yet. I think I'll take another try at it today, and maybe I shall be able in the course of a few days to make out what he means by those *t*'s that look like *w*'s and those *i*'s that haven't any eyebrows."

Other letters are read and thrown away and forgotten; but yours I keep forever—unread. One of them will last a reasonable man a lifetime.

T. B. *Aldrich*

Mark Twain

Mark Twain (Samuel L. Clemens) once said, "A banquet is probably the most fatiguing thing in the world except ditch digging." After a seemingly endless round of banquets, Twain waggishly answered an invitation for dinner from a good friend. As told by Frank Muir in *An Irreverent and Thoroughly Incomplete Social History of Almost Everything*:

Dear Lee:

Can't. I am in a family way with three weeks' undigested dinners in my system, and shall just roost here and diet and purge till I am delivered. Shall I name it after you?

Yr. friend,

Sam'l L. Clemens

H. G. Wells

Author H. G. Wells discovered that he had taken the hat of the mayor of Cambridge, instead of his own. Pleased with his new-found headgear, Wells sent this note to the mayor:

My dear Mayor:

I stole your hat. I like your hat. I shall keep your hat. Whenever I look inside it I shall think of you and your excellent dry sherry, and of the town of Cambridge, which is older than the university. I take off your hat to you.

H. G. *Wells*

Gelett Burgess

That the wit of Gelett Burgess was not confined to *The Purple Cow* was abundantly clear when the *New York Times* referred to him as "the late Mr. Burgess":

To the Editor:

May I venture to protest a mild injustice of which I am the victim in your Sunday issue? I find myself, on the radio page in an article on Dave Elman's Hobby Lobby, referred to as the "late" Gelett Burgess.

Mr. Editor, I am almost never late, even to dinner. I am noted for my promptness in paying my debts, keeping my appointments, and discovering the prettiest gal in the room. In fact, I am an inveterately early bird. Except of course, when it is time to get up in the morning.

I feel confident that in calling me the late G. B. the author was indulging in no phobia or wish fulfillment. Only, my friends ought to know. No flowers, please.

Gelett Burgess

Winston Churchill

When chicken was being served at a dinner in his honor, Winston Churchill asked, "May I have a breast?" His American hostess replied, "In this country it is the custom to ask for white or dark meat." The next day Churchill sent her an orchid with this card:

I would be most obliged if you would pin this on your white meat.

Winston Churchill

Ruth Van Bergen

After taking a portrait of a member of the movie colony, Hollywood photographer Ruth Van Bergen received this complaining note:

Dear Miss Van Bergen:

I am disappointed in my picture. It really isn't very good. The last picture you made of me was simply beautiful.

Name Withheld

Cleverly diplomatic, Miss Van Bergen replied:

Dear Madam:

I agree with you but you must forgive me. The last time I took your picture, I was ten years younger.

Ruth Van Bergen

Vic Gelb

In recent years, clubs like Rotary and Kiwanis opened their memberships to the fair sex. This recalled the letter that business executive Vic Gelb wrote to the Cleveland City Club many years before:

Gentlemen:

I'm appalled by the Board's recent decision to admit women to our traditionally stag Friday Forums . . .

Don't get me wrong. I have nothing against women. Some of my best friends are women. But you've got to draw the line somewhere. Next thing you know they'll be wanting to eat at the same lunch counter with you . . . may even want to move right next door to you. Things may even come to such a point that I wouldn't be surprised if someday my son brought one home and said that he wanted to marry her. Yessir, my friends, if you knock out but just one prop from under the bridge of tradition the whole thing might fall in . . . and then where would we be? This talk about equality can go too far! Next thing you know, some smart-aleck leftist board member is going to suggest that we start operating the Club at a profit!

Vic Gelb

Herman "Fritz" Liebert

Herman "Fritz" Liebert is librarian emeritus of Yale's illustrious Beinecke Rare Book and Manuscript Library. He has also served as chairman of the editorial committee of the Yale edition of Samuel Johnson's works and a member of the editorial committees of the papers of James Boswell and Horace Walpole. When he was notified that the editor of this book had nominated him for honorary membership in the bibliophilic Rowfant Club, Liebert responded:

Dear Jack:

 . . . That it is not yet official I perfectly understand. These things must be done according to the prescribed forms. Perhaps the Rowfanters will proceed in the manner of the Persians, of whom Herodotus tells us that they debated matters of the highest importance twice—once sober and once drunk. . . .

My affectionate regards to you and to all my friends there.

Sincerely,

Fritz

Miss Manners

In *Miss Manners'* (Judith Martin) *Guide to Excruciatingly Correct Behavior*, she explains how a weak smile can be most meaningful:

Dear Miss Manners:

What is the proper reply when someone says, "Excuse me?"

Ann Nonimous

Gentle Reader:

A weak smile. The way to perform a weak smile is to raise the corners of the mouth without moving the center part of the lips, which remain closed. The length of the weak smile depends on the magnitude of the act for which the excuse was requested. For example, if a person has asked to be excused for burping the weak smile in response should last only a fleeting moment, as did the burp, one hopes. If he is asking to be excused for breaking a porcelain vase that your great-grandfather brought back from China, the weak smile becomes fixed. This is to distract attention from the expression in your eyes as you stare at the fragments of china on the floor.

Miss Manners

V

Authors' Wit

T. B. Macaulay
Nathaniel Hawthorne
H. W. Fowler
Henry David Thoreau
James Russell Lowell
John Galsworthy
Sherwood Anderson
Honoré de Balzac
George Bernard Shaw
John Steinbeck
Eugene O'Neill
Arthur C. Clarke
Bernard De Voto
Erle Stanley Gardner
Elliot Paul
Fred Allen
James Michener
P. G. Wodehouse

A single paragraph in an impulsive letter will tell more about a man than a whole work. . .
—*George Jean Nathan*

T. B. Macaulay

A voracious reader, Thomas Babington Macaulay seldom was without a book in his hand. He amusingly wrote a friend of his reading while rambling:

Malverne, August 21st, 1851

Dear Ellis,

. . . the other day I was overtaken by a hearse as I was strolling along and reading the night expedition of Diomede and Ulysses. "Would you like a ride, sir?" said the driver. "Plenty of room." I could not help laughing. "I dare say I shall want such a carriage some day or other. But I am not ready yet." The fellow, with the most consummate professional gravity, answered, "I meant, sir, that there was plenty of room on the box."

I do not think that I ever, at Cambridge or in India, did a better day's work in Greek than today. I have read at one stretch fourteen books of the *Odyssey*, from the Sixth to the Nineteenth inclusive. I did it while walking to Worcester and back.

Ever yours,

T. B. *Macaulay*

Nathaniel Hawthorne

From the Woodrow Wilson International Center for Scholarship came this letter that Nathaniel Hawthorne, as a young man, wrote to his mother:

Dear Mother,

I don't want to be a doctor, and live by men's diseases; nor a minister, to live by their sins; nor a lawyer, to live by their quarrels. So I don't think there's anything left for me but to be an author.

Nathaniel

H. W. Fowler

H. W. Fowler's A *Dictionary of Modern English Usage* still is regarded as one of the best guides to writing. When Fowler's publisher kindly offered to provide him with a servant to ease his latter days, the aging grammarian replied:

6 November 1926

Dear Chapman:

My half-hour from 7 to 7:30 this morning was spent in (1) a two-mile run along the road, (2) a swim in my next-door neighbour's pond. That I am still in condition for such freaks I attribute to having had for nearly 30 years no servants to reduce me to a sedentary and all-literary existence. And now you seem to say: let us give you a servant, and the means of slow suicide and quick lexicography. Not if I know it; I must go my slow way.

H. W. *Folwer*

Henry David Thoreau

Like many of our best writers, Henry David Thoreau, author of the famous *Walden*, was unable to find a publisher for his *A Week on the Concord and Merrimack Rivers*. At his own expense he had a bookseller print one thousand copies. After many months, the dealer returned to Thoreau 706 books still unsold. In this note to himself, in his journal, the great naturalist told why his collection of books was unique among libraries:

Sunday
October 30, 1853

For a year or two past, my *publisher*, falsely so called, has been writing from time to time to ask what disposition should be made of the copies of *A Week on the Concord and Merrimack Rivers* still on hand, and at last suggesting that he had use for the room they occupied in his cellar. So I had them all sent to me here, and they have arrived today by express, filling the man's wagon—706 copies out of an edition of 1,000 which I bought of Munroe four years ago and have been ever since paying for, and have not quite paid for yet. The wares are sent to me at last, and I have an opportunity to examine my purchase. They are something more substantial than fame, as my back knows, which has borne them up two flights of stairs to a place similar to that to which they trace their origin. Of the remaining two hundred and ninety odd, seventy-five were given away, the rest sold. I have now a library of nearly nine hundred volumes, over seven hundred of which I wrote myself. Is it not well that the author should behold the fruits of his labor? My works are piled up on one side of my chamber half as high as my head, my *opera omnia*. This is authorship; these are the work of my brain. . . .

Henry D. Thoreau

James Russell Lowell

A letter from James Russell Lowell to Nathaniel Hawthorne, introducing William Dean Howells, can rightfully be billed as an all-star production. Howells later became Hawthorne's protégé and good friend:

Cambridge, August 6, 1860

My dear Hawthorne:

I have no masonic claims upon you except community of tobacco, and the young man who brings this does not smoke.

But he wants to look at you, which will do you no harm and him a great deal of good.

His name is Howells, and he is a fine young fellow, and has written several poems in the *Atlantic*, which you never read because you don't do such things yourself, and are old enough to know better.... If my judgment is good for anything, this youth has more in him than any of our younger fellows in the way of rhyme...

Yours always,

J. R. *Lowell*

John Galsworthy

Asked by a curious correspondent how a famous author spent his day, John Galsworthy, Nobel prize winner for *The Forsyte Saga*, replied as follows:

August 12, 1927

Analysis of Average Day

Sleeping in bed	7 hours
Thinking in bed	1 hour
Trying not to fall asleep in chairs	1/2 hour
Eating, listening to others talking	1/4 hour
Playing with dogs	1/4 hour
Playing without dogs (on the telephone) ..	1/4 hours
Dressing, undressing, bathing, and Muller exercising	1 1/4 hours
Exercise in country (riding or walking)	2 hours at least
Exercise in London (walking)	1 hour at most
Imagining vain things, and writing them down on paper:	
In the country	4 hours
In London	3 hours
Correspondence, and collecting scattered thoughts:	
In the country	2 hours
In London	4 hours
Skipping newspapers	1/4 hour
Reading what I don't want to, or otherwise attending to business	1 hour
Reading what I do want to	1/2 hour
Revision of vain things; and of proofs, say	1 hour
Education by life	the rest

30-hour day.

Call it an eight or nine-hour day.

J. G.

Sherwood Anderson

When Sherwood Anderson reached the decision to give up his job and devote himself exclusively to writing, he sent his employer this unique letter of resignation:

Chicago
June 25, 1918

Dear Barton:

You have a man in your employ that I have thought for a long time should be fired. I refer to Sherwood Anderson. He is a fellow of a good deal of ability, but for a long time I have been convinced that his heart is not in his work.

There is no question but that this man Anderson has in some ways been an ornament to our organization. His hair, for one thing, being long and mussy, gives an artistic carelessness to his personal appearance that somewhat impresses such men as Frank Lloyd Wright . . .

But Anderson is not really productive. As I have said his heart is not in his work.

I therefore suggest that Anderson be asked to sever his connections with the Company on August 1st. He is a nice fellow. We will let him down easy but let's can him.

Respectfully submitted,

Sherwood Anderson

Honoré de Balzac

Deeply in debt for most of his life, Honoré de Balzac elatedly sent this announcement to his publisher and friends on the death of his miserly uncle who left him a sizeable bequest:

> Yesterday, at five in the morning, my uncle and I passed on to a better life.

> *Balzac*

George Bernard Shaw

Looking over a second-hand book stall, George Bernard Shaw came across a volume of his own plays, which he had given to a friend . . . inscribed on the flyleaf:

With the compliments of

George Bernard Shaw

Shaw bought the book and returned it to his friend with this added note:

With the renewed compliments of

G. B. S.

John Steinbeck

John Steinbeck tells his literary agent that one half of the manuscript for *Of Mice and Men* has been chewed up by his setter pup:

Pacific Grove
May 27, 1936

Dear Miss Otis:

Minor tragedy stalked. I don't know whether I told you. My
setter pup, left alone one night, made confetti of about half of
my ms. book [*Of Mice and Men*]. Two months work to do over
again. It sets me back. There was no other draft. I was pretty
mad but the poor little fellow may have been acting critically. I
didn't want to ruin a good dog for a ms. I'm not sure it is good
at all. He only got an ordinary spanking with his punishment
fly swatter. But there's the work to do over from the start. . . .

I should imagine the new little manuscript will be ready in
about two months. I hope you won't be angry at it. I think it has
something but can't tell much yet.

I'll get this off. I hear the postman.

John Steinbeck

Editor's Note: Many years before, Thomas Carlyle
forgave John Stuart Mill for his housekeeper's accidental burning of the manuscript of *The French Revolution*.

Eugene O'Neill

Traveling in Europe, Eugene O'Neill received a cable from Jean Harlow asking if he would write a play for her. "Reply collect in 20 words," read the cable. O'Neill did:

NO NO NO NO NO NO NO NO NO NO
NO NO NO NO NO NO NO NO NO NO

O'Neill

Arthur C. Clarke

In similar vein, Arthur C. Clarke, author of the science fiction classic *2001: A Space Odyssey*, reports that newspaper tycoon William Randolph Hearst once sent him this message:

Is there life on Mars? Cable thousand words.

Hearst

The scientist cabled:

Nobody knows. Repeat 500 times.

Arthur C. Clarke

Bernard De Voto

After several unsuccessful attempts to persuade author Bernard De Voto to speak before the Civil War Round Table of the Chicago Historical Society, the director of the Society, Paul Angle, made one last try. The editor of Harper's "Easy Chair" replied as follows:

October 26, 1950

Dear Mr. Angle:

... As a literary man, I love to talk about things I'm completely ignorant of, and I do talk about them most of the time, and with great enjoyment. But as a historian, in whatever sense, by God I hold my peace except when I know what I'm talking about. It's only a small decency, but mine own.

I don't know enough about the Civil War to talk to anybody who knows anything about it. Get me up before your audience and I would be seen in all my nakedness within one hundred and twenty seconds ....

Ask me to tell you about Lewis and Clark, or the Welsh Indians, or the Western Sea, or the upper Missouri, and I'll come a-running and talk your heads off. But I'm not fitten to talk about the Civil War and I just can't. Hell, I know more about the War of Jenkins' Ear—not that I know much about that. No, you're very nice to ask me, but I'm a nice guy too; too nice to defraud you with a public show of ignorance.

Sincerely yours,

Bernard De Voto

Erle Stanley Gardner

Before he became famous as the author of "Perry Mason" mysteries, Erle Stanley Gardner sold short stories to *Black Mask* magazine. He submitted one with this note:

Dear Sirs,

"Three O'Clock in the Morning" is a damned good story. If you have any comments, write them on the back of a check.

Erle Stanley Gardner

Elliot Paul

The earliest writing of Elliot Paul, author of *The Last Time I Saw Paris*, was for a Boston newspaper. Discovering they were paying more for *The Adventures of Peter Rabbit*, Paul sent the editor this note:

Dear Sir,

You are robbing Paul to pay Peter.

Elliot Paul

Fred Allen

In this mutual admiration letter from one great humorist to another, Fred Allen hilariously sends his thanks for James Thurber's latest book:

november
19th
1953.

dear james thurber—

i want to thank you for sending me a copy of "thurber country."

my lawyer will see you shortly about the inscription you have kindly added to my copy. you cannot be my greatest admirer since i am your greatest admirer. this is a form of adjective incest rarely practised except by broadway columnists.

many years ago, harold ross wanted to try and make a writer of me. i told harold that when i saw what you were writing i planned to insert my quill back into the fowl.

who knows—if the foot had been on the other shoe— today you might be doing a lousy television program and i might be mailing you a copy of my new book "allen country."

sincerely—

F

James Michener

On several occasions *Time* magazine's book reviewers had downgraded the novels of James Michener. When Michener's *The Source* was published, Michener sent *Time's* editor this quizzical note:

Madrid
June 4, 1965

Dear Editor,

You had me scared for a moment. I thought you might put the whammy on me by liking my latest novel *The Source.* You pooh-poohed *South Pacific* and it became a great hit. You ridiculed *Hawaii* and it was purchased by nearly 4,000,000 readers. You blasted *Caravan* and it stayed near the top of the lists for half a year. Please spell my name right in your Best Seller box in the long months ahead.

James A. Michener

P. G. Wodehouse

P. G. Wodehouse playfully wrote this "goofy" dedication to his daughter in his book *The Heart of a Goof*:

To my daughter Leonora
without whose never-failing sympathy and encouragement
this book would have been finished in half the time.

P. G. Wodehouse

V I

Editors' Wit

Horace Greeley
George Horace Lorimer
William Allen White
H. L. Mencken
Virginia O'Hanlon and Francis P. Church
Richard Watson Gilder
Bernard Kilgore
Harold Ross
Mason Walsh
Newspaper Editor
Paris News
Hugh Montgomery-Massingberd

The proper definition of man is "an animal that writes letters."
—*Lewis Carroll*

Horace Greeley

Antislavery editor and publisher Horace Greeley always maintained that the word "news" was plural. Greeley once sent this query to one of his reporters:

Dear L. A.:

Are there any news?

Horace Greeley

The reporter answered:

Dear Mr. Greeley:

Not a new.

L. A.

George Horace Lorimer

In its early days, the *Saturday Evening Post* ran a serial in which one installment ended with the heroine drinking at night with her married boss in his home, while his wife was away. The following installment began with them having breakfast the next morning. When shocked readers complained, the *Post's* famed editor replied with this letter:

Dear Sir:

The *Post* cannot be responsible for what the characters in its serials do between installments.

George Horace Lorimer

William Allen White

William Allen White was the witty republican editor of the Emporia, Kansas *Gazette*. When a young lady reader asked him for his favorite recipe, this was the sage of Emporia's response:

Dear Miss Edwards:

I have your note asking me for my favorite recipe. Here it is: "Orange au jus."

Take a large ten-cent orange, gouge your thumb in the top, peel without a knife, bust it with the grain, and eat it so, with as much pianissimo on your intake as possible.

William Allen White

H. L. Mencken

H. L. Mencken was co-editor of the *Smart Set* with George Jean Nathan and editor of the *American Mercury*. When William Saroyan expressed a desire to edit a magazine, the ever feisty Mencken sent him this advice:

Dear Saroyan,

I notice what you say about your aspiration to edit a magazine. I am sending you by this mail a six-chambered revolver. Load it and fire every one into your head. You will thank me when you go to hell and learn from other editors there how dreadful their job was on earth.

H. L. Mencken

Virginia O'Hanlon and Francis P. Church

Add to the correspondence destined to live forever that (here much abridged) between eight-year-old Virginia O'Hanlon and the Editor of *The New York Sun*, Francis P. Church:

Dear Editor:

I am eight years old. Some of my little friends say there is no Santa Claus. Papa says, "If you see it in *The Sun* it's so." Please tell me the truth. Is there a Santa Claus?

Virginia O'Hanlon

Dear Virginia:

. . . Yes, Virginia, there is a Santa Claus. He exists as certainly as love and generosity and devotion exist, and you know that they abound and give to our life its highest beauty and joy. Alas! how dreary would be the world if there were no Santa Claus. It would be as dreary as if there were no Virginias. There would be no childlike faith then, no poetry, no romance, to make tolerable this existence. We should have no enjoyment, except in sense and sight. The eternal light with which childhood fills the world would be extinguished.

Not believe in Santa Claus! You might as well not believe in fairies! . . . Did you ever see fairies dancing on the lawn? Of course not, but that's no proof that they are not there. Nobody can conceive or imagine all the wonders there are unseen and unseenable in the world. . . .

No Santa Claus? Thank God! he lives, and he lives forever. A thousand years from now, Virginia, nay, ten times ten thousand years from now, he will continue to make glad the heart of childhood.

Your Editor

Richard Watson Gilder

When Mark Twain traveled to London on a lecture tour, his address was not generally known. When a reader asked *Century Magazine* how Twain could be reached, editor Gilder complied with an amusing anecdote:

December 9, 1897.

Dear Mr. T———:

Mark Twain can be addressed, care of Messrs. Chatto & Windus, 111 St. Martin's Lane, London, W. C. I would say that a letter was addressed to him some time ago (before people knew the Chatto & Windus address) "God Knows Where," and it found him. I tried the address "The Devil Knows Where," and this also reached him; so it seems that he is known at "both concerns."

Richard Watson Gilder

Bernard Kilgore

In this memo to his staff, Bernard Kilgore, erstwhile chairman of *The Wall Street Journal*, orders the banning of one of his pet aversions:

Notice To All Editors

From: Bernard Kilgore, Chairman

LANG

If I see the word upcoming in *The Wall Street Journal* once more, I shall be downcoming on someone who will be outgoing.

Harold Ross

One of the quirkiest of editors was Harold Ross of *The New Yorker*. When Charles Cooke wrote a piece about a dog, saying, "He stared at us and smiled affably," Ross dashed off this note to his managing editor:

McKelway,

Tell Cooke for God's sake stop attributing human behavior to dogs. The dog may have stared but Cooke knows damn well he didn't smile.

Ross

McKelway sent the memo to Cooke with this note:

Cooke,

Ross wants you to for God's sake stop attributing human behavior to dogs. O.K.?

McK

Cooke replied,

O, for God's sake, K.

C. C.

Later that day Cooke got this message:

Ross says your dog piece is swell. He put it through as it is and left in the smile. Bow for God's sake wow.

McK

Mason Walsh

The AP *Log*, weekly bulletin of the Associated Press, intercepted the following communication to a Houston editor from a Dallas ditto:

DALLAS TIMES HERALD
DALLAS, TEXAS

Roderick J. Watts
Houston Chronicle
Houston, Texas

Dear Watts:

Punctuation marks (.,:;?" ') are important. My favorite is the period (.) which is used less often than it should be. Many a sentence could be nailed down earlier in its career by a period (.). Too many writers keep tossing in a comma (,) here, a comma (,) there. The result is a succession of comma-specked sentences that bulge with unnecessary words and phrases.

But I'm not writing about periods (....) or commas (,,,,). My target is the quotation mark ("), the overuse of this punctuation, and such overuse in the AP report.

Any punctuation mark (.,:;?" ') slows the reader. He has to step over them, go around them, or back up and jump past them. In some quote-coated AP stories, he is breathless by the time he finaly arrives at that welcome period (.). In exhaustion, he may never complete the sentence.

Don't misunderstand me. I believe in punctuation marks (.,:;?" '). I believe the quotation mark (") is here to stay. But a story peppered with too many quotation marks (" " " ") can be indigestible.

Direct quotation frequently can add much to a story. But what is the point in breaking out in a rash of quotation marks (" " ") around one, two, three, or a dozen words?

Mason Walsh

Newspaper Editor

Edward Frank Allen in his book on *Effective English* quotes this bulletin from a managing editor of an eastern newspaper to his reportorial staff:

To All Reporters:

We do not commence, we begin. We do not purchase, we buy. We do not pass away, we die. We are buried in coffins, not caskets. We are not all gentlemen, but we are all men. All women are not ladies, but all women are women. All women are female, it is true, but dogs, horses, and pigs can also be female: hence, in deference to our women, we shall not class them as mere "females." We do not reside in residences, we live in homes. We do not retire, we go to bed. Our priests, ministers, and rabbis are not divines. Our lawyers are not barristers. Our undertakers are not morticians. Our real estate dealers are not realtors. Our plumbers are not sanitary engineers. Our cobblers are not shoe rebuilders. All fires are not conflagrations. And the first reporter who writes of a body landing "with a dull-sickening thud," will land with a dull-sickening thud in the street, with hat in one hand and pay envelope in the other.

Managing Editor

Paris News

The editor of the *Farm Journal* was on the complimentary list to receive free copies of many publications. One newspaper arrived with this note attached:

Paris, Texas

Dear Editor,

ST   Because of the increased cost of printing and mailing, taxes, and inflation, this publication comes to you twice as free as it used to.

Paris News

Hugh Montgomery-Massingberd

After *Time* magazine called Burke's Peerage directories "snob's bibles," they received this chiding note from Burke's editor in London.

Burke's Peerage Ltd.
London

Dear Sirs,

Our books are scholarly records of social history, not "snob's bibles." If you do not believe this, try reading one— without prejudice. You will be surprised. Indeed, your flabber will never have been so gasted.

LANG

Hugh Montgomery-Massingberd
Editorial Director

VII

Publisher's Wit

Aldus Manutius
Victor Hugo
Edna St. Vincent Millay
A. C. Fifield
M. Lincoln Schuster
Bennett Cerf
Groucho Marx
Jack London
Unknown Author
Paul Brooks
Lynn Caine
Don Quinn
Mary Busy
Alfred A. Knopf

There are no walls in letters. The words fly out of
your heart
—*Anne Sexton*

DEAR WIT

Aldus Manutius

Aldus Manutius, the famed sixteenth-century publisher of fine books, complains of interruptions and posts rules for visitors to his Aldine Press:

Aldus Manutius to Navagerus:

I am hampered in my work by a thousand interruptions. Nearly every hour comes a letter from some scholar, and if I undertook to reply to them all, I should be obliged to devote day and night to scribbling. Then through the day come calls from all kinds of visitors. . . .

Even these people with no business are not so bad as those who have a poem to offer or something in prose (usually very prosy indeed) that they wish to see printed with the name of Aldus. These interruptions are now becoming too serious for me, and I must take steps to lessen them.

As a warning to the heedless visitors who use up my office hours to no purpose, I have now put up a big notice on the door of my office to the following effect:

WHOEVER THOU ART, THOU ART EARNESTLY REQUESTED BY ALDUS

TO STATE THY BUSINESS BRIEFLY

AND TO TAKE THY DEPARTURE PROMPTLY.

IN THIS WAY THOU MAYST BE OF SERVICE

EVEN AS WAS HERCULES TO THE WEARY ATLAS,

FOR THIS IS A PLACE OF WORK

FOR ALL WHO MAY ENTER.

Aldus

Victor Hugo

M. Lincoln Schuster considered this wordless exchange one of the classic brevities of his extensive letter collection. Shortly after *The Hunchback of Notre Dame* was published, Victor Hugo wrote his publisher to find out how sales were going:

Dear Paul:

?

Victor Hugo

The editor replied:

Dear Victor:

!

Paul

Edna St. Vincent Millay

After rejecting a suggestion from her publisher for boosting the sale of one of her books, poetess Edna St. Vincent Millay offered this parting quip:

Dear Mr. Canfield:

... Trusting that it may be said of me by Harper & Brothers that, although I reject their proposals, I welcome their advances.

Edna St. Vincent Millay

A. C. Fifield

Gertrude Stein once submitted a manuscript to British publisher A. C. Fifield who was unimpressed by the Stein repetitive style. ("Rose is a rose is a rose.") The publisher rejected the work with this parody:

13, Clifford's Inn
London, E. C.
April 19, 1912

Dear Madam,

I am only one, only one, only one. Only one being, one at the same time. Not two, not three, only one. Only one life to live, only sixty minutes in one hour. Only one pair of eyes. Only one brain. Only one being. Being only one, having only one pair of eyes, having only one time, having only one life, I cannot read your MS three or four times. Not even one time. Only one look, only one look is enough. Hardly one copy would sell here. Hardly one. Hardly one.

Many thanks. I am returning the MS by registered post. Only one MS by one post.

A. C. Fifield

M. Lincoln Schuster

A budding young author inquired of publishers Simon and Schuster:

Gentlemen,

How big an advance will you offer for a novel of 60,000 words?

R——— C———

Schuster promptly replied, with this query:

Dear Sir,

How big are the words?

M. *Lincoln Schuster*

Bennett Cerf

Bennett Cerf, of Random House, was Gertrude Stein's publisher. Confessing that he was "bewildered by her writing," he printed this note on the jacket of one of Stein's books:

PUBLISHER'S NOTE

This space is usually reserved for a brief description of a book's contents. In this case, however, I must admit frankly that I do not know what Miss Stein is talking about. I do not even understand the title.

I admire Miss Stein tremendously, and I like to publish her books, although most of the time I do not know what she is driving at. That, Miss Stein tells me, is because I am dumb.

I note that one of my partners and I are characters in this latest work of Miss Stein's. Both of us wish that we knew what she was saying about us. Both of us hope, too, that her faithful followers will make more of this book than we are able to!

Bennett Cerf

Groucho Marx

"the blurbers)-

William Cole spent fifteen years soliciting jacket blurbs from notables praising books published by Alfred A. Knopf and Simon & Schuster. He reports that this is how Groucho Marx responded when Cole sent him a book of humor:

Dear Sir,

I've been laughing ever since I picked up your book. Some day I'm going to read it.

Groucho

Jack London

When failing two weeks in a row to meet his contract to furnish a story, Jack London received this ultimatum from his publisher. This exchange also has been attributed to O. Henry:

My dear Jack London:

> If I do not receive those stories from you by noon tomorrow, I'm going to put on my heaviest soled shoes, come down to your room, and kick you downstairs. I always keep my promises.

Editor

The author of *Call of the Wild* replied:

Dear Sir,

> I, too, would always keep my promises if I could fulfill them with my feet.

Jack London

Unknown Author

Unsuccessful in getting larger royalties to meet the mounting costs of living, a Los Angeles author wrote his publisher as follows:

Dear Sirs:

> I have changed the name of the miserable little checks you send me from "royalties" to "peasantries."

Name Withheld

Paul Brooks

Paul Brooks, editor of Houghton Mifflin Company, suggests that this might be a suitable reply for a publisher to send to a literary agent who has been overzealous in guarding his author's interests:

Dear Sir:

I have your letter declaring that you will examine our contract with suspicion. For your guidance, it is only fair that I give you the following pointers:

1.   Our technicians at the Riverside Press have recently evolved a clever overlay under which we customarily conceal the most important clauses in our contracts. When this is later removed by the Publisher in the privacy of his closet, the contract is revealed to mean precisely the opposite to what appears on the surface.

2.   A line of diamond type, appearing to the casual reader like a displaced printer's lead (near the phrase "Heirs and Assigns"), gives the Publisher the right to pay the author in dollars Mex. or in Chinese currency, as the Publisher may determine.

3.   On page four there is a paragraph written in lemon juice giving the Publisher 100% (one hundred percent) of receipts from motion picture sales.

4.   All references to advances or royalties are typed in a cheese-like emulsion attractive to mice; they invariably disappear after the contract has been for some time in our files.

Sincerely yours,

Paul Brooks

Lynn Caine

Outraged by the Dial Press' publication of A *Cat-Hater's Handbook* by William Cole, Lynn Caine of Farrar, Straus addressed this note of protest to the rival publishing firm:

January 25, 1963

Mr. James Silberman
The Dial Press
New York 16, New York

Dear Jim:

Shame on you for publishing A *Cat-Hater's Handbook* by William Cur [sic]. More shame on you for compounding the feliny [sic] by failing to research his facts. Though it is true that many derogatory terms embrace the word "cat," it is untrue that no other animal has inspired so distasteful a collection of denigratory expressions. Omitting such obvious and unsportsmanlike animals as the pig, the ape, and the ass, let's consider derogatory dog terms.

One definition is, of course, a "low, contemptible fellow." Then there's the slang expression for savage, ruthless competition, "dog eat dog." There's that unlikeable man who keeps others from using that which he cannot use, the "dog in the manger." People who have "gone to the dogs" don't earn my respect, nor do idlers, who "dog away the time."

... What's more deplorable than badly constructed verse, "doggerel"? And, finally, how do we in the trade describe a bad book? What else? A dog. Nothing personal.

Sincerely,

Lynn Caine
Director of Publicity

Don Quinn

A best-selling author received this letter from a humorist-writer who bought a copy of his book—cleverly protesting against the eye-straining type in which the book was set:

Dear Sir:

I bought your new book last night and I hope I'll enjoy it as much as I—and the world— did your last one. If I do, I'll have my seeing eye dog bring me over to tell you, and believe me, if I get through this book I'll need a hound with 20/20 vision and a tolerant disposition. I'd like to make a suggestion for future editions. Knopf used to do it and what has Knopf got that your publishers haven't except maybe Garamond and Bodoni? Here:

A NOTE ON THE TYPE IN WHICH THIS BOOK WAS SET

The type used in this volume is known, quite unfavorably, as 1/2-point Myopia, and was designed in 1622 by Feodor Astigmatism, the Elder. It was deciphered in 1944 by means of the electron microscope and bids fair to become one of the most heartily disliked faces this side of Francisco Franco. We predict that it will be used extensively for engraving the text of Magna Charta on the edges of scalpels and to inscribe messages of love and devotion on gold toothpicks and stick-pins presented to producers . . .

Don Quinn

Mary Busy

After granting the request of young writer Mary Busy for an introduction to Macmillan's, James Michener, blockbuster author, received this thank-you note:

Dear Mr. Michener:

> I have definite proof that your note of introduction stood me in good stead. Macmillan now rejects my manuscripts on a much finer grade of stationery.

> *Mary Busy*

Alfred A. Knopf

Bennett Cerf reported that book publisher Alfred A. Knopf received an unsolicited manuscript with this note attached:

Gentlemen:

> Please tell me as soon as possible if you think my brainchild is Knopfable.

> *Name Withheld*

The reply was short and final:

Dear Sir:

> Kno.

> *Alfred A. Knopf*

VIII

Autographic Wit

Rudyard Kipling
Madame Marie Curie
Mark Twain
George Bernard Shaw
John F. Kennedy
Peter De Vries

Autographs are the most fascinating of all collected things.
—*Thomas F. Madigan*

Rudyard Kipling

Gene Perret, in *Writer's Digest*, reports that Rudyard Kipling was paid five dollars per word by *Ladies' Home Journal* for his "Just So Stories": A crafty autograph collector sent Kipling five dollars and asked for a word. The noted author replied:

Dear Sir,

Thanks.

Rudyard Kipling

The collector triumphantly answered:

Dear Mr. Kipling,

I sold the story of your one-word reply to a magazine for two hundred dollars. The enclosed check is your half.

The Humorist of Fleet Street

Madame Marie Curie

Madame Marie Curie, double Nobel-Prize-winning discoverer of radium, refused to patent her process and to profit from it in any way. Knowing that she refused to give autographs, a collector sent her a check for twenty-five dollars expecting to receive her endorsement on the cancelled check. Not deceived by this subterfuge, Madame Curie instructed her secretary to send the following:

Dear Sir,

Madame Curie has asked me to thank you most kindly for your check, which, however, she is not going to cash. It so happens that she is an autograph collector and therefore will add your signature to her collection.

Secretary to Madame Curie

Mark Twain

When Edward Bok, great reformer, publisher, and collector, requested Mark Twain's autograph, he received this reply. A fine example of Twain's merciless wit, yet because the whole letter, including the signature, was typewritten, its value as a collector's item was greatly reduced:

Dear Sir:

I hope I shall not offend you; I shall certainly say nothing with the intention to offend you. . . . What you ask me to do, I am asked to do as often as one-half dozen times a week. Three hundred times a year! One's impulse is to freely consent, but one's time and necessary occupations will not permit it. There is no way but to decline in all cases, making no exceptions, and I wish to call your attention to a thing which has probably not occurred to you, and that is this: that no man takes pleasure in exercising his trade as a pastime. Writing is my trade, and I exercise it only when I am obliged to. You might make your request of a doctor, or a builder, or a sculptor, and there would be no impropriety in it, but if you asked either of those for a specimen of his trade, his handiwork, he would be justified in rising to a point of order. It would never be fair to ask a doctor for one of his corpses to remember him by.

Mark Twain

George Bernard Shaw

When George Bernard Shaw once boasted in an article that he knew how to brew the perfect cup of coffee, a country parson wrote to him for the recipe. Shaw sent it to him but with this note appended:

> I hope that this is a genuine request and not a surreptitious mode of securing my autograph.

> G. B. S.

To which the country parson replied:

Dear Mr. Shaw:

> Accept my thanks for the recipe. I wrote in good faith, so allow me to return what it is obvious you infinitely prize, but which is of no value to me—your autograph.

> *Country Parson*

John F. Kennedy

Columnist Leonard Lyons once wrote to John F. Kennedy, reporting these prices for signed presidential photos which he spotted in a New York window display: George Washington, $175; Franklin D. Roosevelt, $75; Ulysses S. Grant, $55; John F. Kennedy, $65. Lyons received this unsigned reply:

Dear Leonard:

   I appreciate your letter about the market on Kennedy signatures. It is hard to believe that the going price is so high now. In order not to depress the market any further, I will not sign this letter.

Peter De Vries

Hugh Moorhead was an ingenious autograph collector. He sent authors copies of their own books and asked them to inscribe them with an answer to the riddle, "What is the meaning of life?" Author Peter De Vries complied with the following:

   The universe is like a safe to which there is a combination. But the combination is locked up in the safe.
   Still we keep asking, wistfully and eternally, "why?"

Peter De Vries

I X

Rhetorical Wit

Dorothy Osborne
Robert Burns
George Courteline
Minnie Maddern Fiske
Unnamed Author
S. McPherson
Raymond Chandler
Winston Churchhill
Typogragher
Julian S. Huxley
Bergen Evans
Lester P. Aurbach
Arthur Kudner
B. M. Starks
Marian Forer
Dizzy Dean

Naturalness is the very passport of admission to the company of good letter writing.
—*George Saintsbury*

Dorothy Osborne

Dorothy Osborne, famed seventeenth-century letter writer, explains to Sir William Temple why she favors simplicity and naturalness over the stilted style which characterized letter writing in her times:

September, 1653

Sir,

ON LETTER WRI (handwritten)

In my opinion . . . great scholars are not the best writers (of letters, I mean) . . .

All letters, methinks, should be free and easy as one's discourse; not studied as an oration, nor made up of hard words like a charm. 'Tis an admirable thing to see how some people will labour to find out terms that may obscure a plain sense. Like a gentleman I know, who would never say "the weather grew cold," but that "winter began to salute us." I have no patience for such coxcombs, and cannot blame an old uncle of mine that threw the standish at his man's head because he writ a letter for him where, instead of saying (as his master bid him), "that he would have writ himself, but he had the gout in his hand," he said, "that the gout in his hand would not permit him to put pen to paper." The fellow thought he had mended it mightily, and that putting pen to paper was much better than plain writing.

Dorothy Osborne

Robert Burns

Exasperated by an unfavorable review by an unidentified critic, the famed author of many poems in Scottish dialect shows that he also mastered the art of English vituperation:

Circa 1791

Dear Sir:

. . . Thou eunuch of language: thou butcher, imbruing thy hands in the bowels of orthography: thou arch-heretic in pronunciation: thou pitch-pipe of affected emphasis: thou carpenter, mortising the awkward joints of jarring sentences: thou squeaking dissonance of cadence; thou pimp of gender: thou scape-gallows from the land of syntax: thou scavenger of mood and tense: thou murderous accoucheur of infant learnings: thou ignis fatuus, misleading the steps of benighted ignorance: thou pickle-herring in the puppet-show of nonsense. . . .

Robert Burns

Georges Courteline

An impudent, young writer sent a crude note filled with misspellings to French playwright Georges Courteline, demanding satisfaction for a minor insult. This was the satiric dramatist's reply:

My dear young sir:

As I am the offended party, the choice of weapons is mine. We shall fight with orthography. You are already dead.

Georges Courteline

Minnie Maddern Fiske

After a performance of *The Rivals*, leading actress Minnie Maddern Fiske found this note stuck in the mirror of her dressing table:

> Margaret Anglin says Mrs. Fiske is the best actress in America.

PUN

Mrs. Fiske hastily inserted two commas and returned the note to actress Margaret Anglin, so that it read:

AMBIG

> Margaret Anglin, says Mrs. Fiske, is the best actress in America.

Unnamed Author

In an article in a widely-read magazine, an Indian maharani was described as wearing a sarong instead of a sari. The red-faced author hastened to send this unsigned note to the editor:

Dear Editor:

> All I can say is I'm sari I was sarong.

PUN

Unnamed Author

S. McPherson

Before leaving India, a Scotsman was asked for a letter of recommendation by his Muslim manservant. Recalling the regularity with which his rupees and other belongings had disappeared, the Scotsman dashed off this note:

To Whom It May Concern:

The bearer of this note, Raju Ram, has served me during the last two years to complete satisfaction. If you are thinking of giving him a berth, be sure to make it a wide one.

S. McPherson

Raymond Chandler

When mystery author Raymond Chandler received blue-pencilled proofs of an article he had written for the *Atlantic Monthly*, he dashed off this sizzling note to editor Edward Weeks:

Dear Weeks:

. . . Would you convey my compliments to the purist who reads your proofs and tell him or her that I write in a sort of broken-down patois which is something like the way a Swiss waiter talks, and that when I split an infinitive, damn it, I split it so it will stay split, and when I interrupt the velvety smoothness of my more or less literate syntax with a few sudden words of barroom vernacular, this is done with the eyes wide open and the mind relaxed but attentive. The method may not be perfect, but it is all I have.

Raymond Chandler

Winston Churchill

"In selecting a best or favorite of about anything," wrote Judge Carl D. Friebolin, "the selector's judgment can not be impeached; it's a subjective reaction. As Milt Gross once said, 'If you like it, you like it—that's all there's to it.'" Judge Friebolin's favorite is the note Winston Churchill once addressed to the British Foreign Office, after a speech had been returned to him with no comment except for the correction of a sentence ending in a preposition:

Sirs:

This is the type of arrant pedantry up with which I will not put.

Churchill

Typographer

A typographer sent this clever example of his art as a Christmas card to his teenage daughter . . . proving that sometimes punctuation marks can be more expressive than words:

Girls who eat their spinach have legs like this: !!
Girls who ride horseback have legs like this: ()
Girls who get drunk have legs like this:)(
And girls who use good judgment have legs like this: X

Julian S. Huxley

Julian S. Huxley, zoologist and grandson of Thomas Huxley, the famous Darwinist, sought everywhere for the correct plural of rhinoceros. Finally, admitting defeat, he addressed this letter to the *Times* of London:

August 17, 1938

Sir,

In your issue of July 30 you employed *rhinoceri* as the plural of rhinoceros. This is surely a barbarism, although on referring to the *New Oxford Dictionary* I find to my surprise and regret that it is one of the usages cited.

This plural has given writers of English considerable trouble. Besides rhinoceros, rhinoceroses, and the above-mentioned rhinoceri, the N.E.D. quotes rhinocerons, rhinoceroes, rhinocerotes, and rhinocerontes.

Rhinoceroses would appear to be the least objectionable, but even this still has a pedantic sound. Has not the time come when we can discard our etymological prejudices, accept ℒ PEₐ the usage of the ordinary man, and frankly use "rhinos"?. . .

Yours faithfully,

Julian S. Huxley

Bergen Evans

Bergen Evans once received a letter from Groucho Marx asking him to discuss the inanity of the cringing, archaic phrase: "I beg to remain." Word expert Evans replied:

April 18, 1959

Dear Groucho,

"I beg to remain" is a piece of detritus from the days when a merchant was expected to show his inferiority to his customers. A book of instructions for the young shopkeeper in the eighteenth century tells him that he must "be master of a handsome bow and cringe." "I beg to remain" is part of the cringe. English tailors will keep it. It's part of what Max Beerbohm called "crawling on their knees and shaking their fist in your face." And I suppose it was an improvement on "Your humble and obedient servant." Now *there* was a subscription! Samuel Johnson, in that wonderful and terrible letter to Chesterfield—after he had the noble lord by the weazand and then kicked him squarely . . . three or four times—solemnly signed himself "Your Lordship's most humble, most obedient servant." For a parallel to *that* sort of humility, the world had to wait for Arthur Godfrey.

Best wishes,

Bergen Evans

Lester P. Aurbach

Lester Aurbach, late president of the Industrial Publishing Company, spotted this witty anecdote told of Mrs. Chauncey Depew, wife of the noted after-dinner speaker, by Abram Sachar of Brandeis University:

May 10, 1984

Dear Jack,

We have all become accustomed to the use of words to obfuscate and misdirect. But once in a while in this veil of tears we can find a ray of light—a kindness—through the use of phrases that lighten our burdens. As witness: the story told of Mrs. Chauncey Depew, one of America's wealthiest women, who decided that she would like to have a family tree developed. In the conference with the genealogist she is said to have told him that unfortunately one of her immediate ancestors—Uncle [Nameless]—had been punished for his final crime by being electrocuted at Sing Sing. Said the genealogist—"Don't worry, I'll take care of Uncle [Nameless]."

He wrote:

"Uncle [Nameless] occupied a chair of applied electricity in one of the government's greatest institutions. He died in harness and his death came as an extreme shock."

Best regards,

Lester P. Aurbach

Arthur Kudner

Arthur Kudner, prominent advertising executive, knew the art of good copywriting. He once penned these words of advice to his son:

Dear Son,

> Never fear big long words.
> Big long words name little things.
> All big things have little names—
> Such as life and death, peace and war.
> Or dawn, day, night, hope, love, home.
> Learn to use little words in a big way—
> It is hard to do
> But they say what you mean.
> When you don't know what you mean—
> Use big words.
> That often fools little people.

Arthur Kudner

B. M. Starks

After reading in *Time* that oft-dated Countess Beatty quarreled with Frank Sinatra and drove off in a small British auto, whimsically called a Huff, a Kentucky reader addressed this letter to the editor:

Louisville, Ky.

Sir:

You repeated that Lady Beatty spatted with Sinatra and "drove off in a Huff." It was not a Huff, but a Dudgeon. It is easy to understand how this mistake was made. It was not one of the oldmodel high Dudgeons, but one of the new low ones, which are frequently mistaken for Huffs, particularly when there is any fog about. I am quite sure of the facts in this matter, as I happened to be driving by in my 1958 Dilemma at the time.

B. M. *Starks*

Marian Forer

John G. Fuller, who liked to discuss the play of words in his *Saturday Review* column, "Trade Winds," received this novel suggestion from one of his readers:

Winnipeg, Manitoba
Canada

July 30, 1964

Dear Mr. Fuller:

I was struck (lightly) the other day by the following wonder: if lawyers become disbarred, and priests are unfrocked, how might people in other paths of life be read out of their profession or calling?

It occurred to me then that electricians get delighted . . . and musicians possibly denoted. If these assumptions are correct, surely it follows that cowboys must be deranged, that models are deposed, and judges are obviously distorted. A medium who loses her license is dispirited and . . . it seems only poetic justice then that a Far Easterner who is banished is disoriented.

I could go on and on, but I don't want to overload the mail handlers. An office worker who can't cope may, alas, become defiled.

Yours sincerely,

Marian Forer

WORD
PLAY

Dizzy Dean

Dizzy Dean was a baseball great, but well known for his poor grammar. Once when a group of teachers criticized him for using "ain't," Dean replied:

Dear Ladies,

There are a lot of school teachers who ain't using ain't—but they ain't eating.

Dizzy Dean

X

Poetic Wit

John Donne
Alexander Pope
Yuan Mei
W. M. Thackeray
Algernon Swinburne
Lewis Carroll
Eugene Field
James Whitcomb Riley
Noel Coward and Gertrude Lawrence
Ben D. Zevin
CBS Staffer

Letters are the world's unwritten sonnets.
—*Christopher Morley*

John Donne

John Donne, sixteenth- and early seventeenth-century poet and dean of St. Paul, was secretary to Sir Thomas Egerton, keeper of the Great Seal. He eloped with Sir Thomas's fourteen-year-old niece, Ann Moore, without her parents' required consent. Imprisoned, Donne sent this cryptic note to his bride:

Anne,

> John Donne, Anne Done, Undone.

John

Alexander Pope

Alexander Pope's translation of Homer's *Iliad* and *Odyssey*, preserved in the British Museum, was written in hundreds of pieces, on the back of architectural plans, household bills, and letters from Steele and Addison; one piece was used to wrap a gift of cherries as this letter testifies:

Teresa and Margaret Blount

Dear Ladies:

> You have here all the fruit Mr. Dancastle's garden affords, that I could find In any degree of ripeness. They were on the trees at eleven o'clock this morning, and I hope will be with you before night. Pray return, sealed up by the bearer, every single bit of paper that wraps them up; for they are the only copies of this part of *Homer*. If the fruit is not as good as I wish, let the gallantry of this wrapping paper make up for it: I am yours . . .

Alexander Pope

Yuan Mei

After receiving an award for his verses, Yuan Mei, the eighteenth-century Chinese poet explains, in his own charming way, that he is reluctantly exchanging a stanza for a tobacco pouch:

Dear Friend:

I have received your letter of congratulations, and am much obliged. At the end of the letter, however, you mention that you have a tobacco-pouch for me, which will be forwarded upon the receipt of a stanza. But such an exchange would seem to establish a curious precedent. If for a tobacco-pouch you expect in return a stanza, for a hat or a pair of boots you would demand a whole poem; while your brother might bestow a cloak or coat upon me, and believe himself entitled to an epic. At this rate, dear friend, your congratulations would become rather costly to me.

Let me instruct you, on the other hand, that a man once gave a thousand yards of silk for a phrase, and another man a beautiful girl for a stanza—which makes your tobacco-pouch look like a slight inducement, does it not? .   .   .

Now, if you had taken needle and thread and made the pouch yourself—ah, then what a difference! Then, indeed, a dozen stanzas would not have been too great a return. But it would hardly be proper to ask a famous warrior like yourself to lay down sword and shield for needle and thread. Nor, dear friend, am I likely to get the pouch at all, if you take offense at these little jokes of mine. What I advise you to do is to bear with me patiently, send the tobacco-pouch, and wait for the stanza until it comes.

Yuan Mei

W. M. Thackeray

Aways wanting to edit a literary journal, William Makepeace Thackeray established the _Cornhill Magazine_. Thackeray published poems of Elizabeth Barrett Browning, but found it necessary to turn down one of her verses in this masterpiece of diplomacy:

My dear, kind Mrs. Browning:

Has Browning ever had an aching tooth which must come out (I don't say Mrs. Browning, for women are much more courageous)—a tooth which must come out, and which he has kept for months and months away from the dentist? I have had such a tooth a long time, and have sat down in this chair, and never had the courage to undergo the pull.

This tooth is an allergory (I mean _this_ one). It's your poem that you sent me months ago, and who am I to refuse the poems of Elizabeth Browning and set myself up as a judge over her? . . .

In your poem, you know, there is an account of unlawful passion, felt by a man for a woman, and though you write pure doctrine, and real modesty, and pure ethics, I am sure our readers would make an outcry, and so I have not published this poem.

To have to say no to my betters is one of the hardest duties I have, but I'm sure we must not publish your verses, and I go down on my knees before cutting my victim's head off, and say, "Madam, you know how I respect and regard you, Browning's wife and Penini's mother; and for what I am going to do I most humbly ask your pardon."

I am, dear Mrs. Browning,

Always yours,

W. M. _Thackeray_

Algernon Swinburne

Failing to interest any publisher in his *Rubaiyat of Omar Khayyam*, Edward Fitzgerald had it printed at his own expense in a small quarto pamphlet. Finding no buyers at its price of half a crown, bookseller Bernard Quaritch placed the pamphlets in "the penny box outside his door." Swinburne tells what happened next, in this letter to A. C. Benson:

Dear Benson,

Neither Burton nor Rossetti nor I have had anything to do with the discovery of Edward Fitzgerald . . . . Two friends of Rossetti's—Mr. Whitley Stokes and Mr. Ormsby—told him (he told me) of this wonderful little pamphlet for sale on a stall (in St. Martin's Lane if you know where that is) to which Mr. Quaritch, finding that the British public unanimously declined to give a shilling for it, had relegated it to be disposed of for a penny. Having read it, Rossetti and I invested upwards of six-pence apiece—or possibly threepence—I would not wish to exaggerate our extravagance—in copies at that not exorbitant price. Next day we thought we might get some more for presents among friends—but the man at the stall asked two-pence! Rossetti expostulated with him in terms of such humorously indignant remonstrance as none but he could ever have commanded. We took a few, and left him. In a week or two, if I am not mistaken, the remaining copies were sold at a guinea; I have since—as I dare say you have—seen copies for still more absurd prices. I kept my own pennyworth (the tidiest copy of the lot) and have it still.

Algernon Swinburne

Editor's Note: This same little pamphlet is worth many thousands of dollars today, according to Alice Loranth, curator of the John G. White Collection of the Cleveland Public Library.

Lewis Carroll

Lewis Carroll (Charles Lutwidge Dodgson), who wrote *Alice's Adventures in Wonderland* for his youngster-friend Alice Liddell, wrote many enchanting letters to other little girls. When small Maggie Cunningham asked him to write a verse for her, the master of nonsense sent this rhymed reply:

April 10, 1871

No, No! I cannot write a line,
    I cannot write a word:
The thoughts I think appear in ink
    So shockingly absurd.

To wander in an empty cave
    Is fruitless work, 'tis said:
What it must be for one like me
    To wander in his head?

You say that I'm "to write a verse"
    Oh Maggie, put it quite
The other way, and kindly say
    That I'm "averse to write!"

CD

Eugene Field

When poet Eugene Field was writing the newspaper column, "Sharps and Flats," he included these rhymed words satirizing hypocritical words used to sign off unfriendly letters:

An Editor in Kankakee,

Falling in a burning passion
with a vexatious rival, he

Wrote him a letter in this fashion:

Sir:

You are an ass, uncouth and rude,
And will be one eternally.

(Then in absent-minded mood
He signed it)

Yours fraternally.

James Whitcomb Riley

James Whitcomb Riley, "The Untamed Hoosier," composed poems like "Little Orphant Annie" for the Indianapolis Journal. When hounded by the editor for a verse, Riley wrote:

Mr. Editor—

    "Why in thunder don't you answer my letter?" says you. 'Cause, b'Gawd, your "letter" was a demand for a poem, and I hain't got one to my back, nor the time to write one! That's what you want to cuss about, and how can I help myself! I can't begin to write poems as fast as I'm asked for 'em; if I could, you'd get one instead of this apology to go on cussin' about. I'm sorry, but it's just that way—so what's a fellow to do? "Every man stretches his legs according to the length of his coverlet," says good Chispa, so be very lenient with the little bench-legg'd poet who has the audacity to sign himself,

Your friend,

James Whitcomb Riley

Noel Coward and Gertrude Lawrence

On Gertrude Lawrence's wedding day she received this congratulatory salute from Noel Coward:

Dear Mrs. A.—

> Hooray, hooray! At last you are deflowered!
> On this as every other day I love you.

—Noel Coward

Not to be outdone, the leading lady of *Lady in the Dark*, responded in her own doggerel:

Dear Mr. C.—

You know me, my parts I overact 'em.
As for the flowers, we searched for hours,
  my maid she must have packed 'em.

—Gertrude Lawrence

Ben D. Zevin

Joe Newman, witty lyricist, versifier, and columnist, once upbraided book publishers for promoting novelists Alec Waugh and Herman Wouk instead of poets. Ben D. Zevin, then head of the World Publishing Co., who had published two Newman books of verse, sent this rhymed comment:

I swear that I will never see
A poet Whittier than thee!
Why should I publish Nash or Truman
When no one sends me quite like Newman,
And Viking, Knopf, and Lippincott
All envy me the poet I've got?
Not even Winnie and his garter
Could ever dim my unleashed ardor,
Nor any future Wouks or Waugh,
Nor all the rights to G. B. Shaw.
No other bard excites my loyalty
Wha'dya want? More lousy royalty?

L'Envoi

Nay, Joe, I haven't thee forsook;
Get busy . . . write another book!

Ben

CBS Staffer

When Laurence Tisch took over Columbia Broadcasting System, he had the choice of cutting costs or selling off CBS divisions to pay off debts incurred by the takeover. Tisch chose the former method, which inspired this parody of "The Night Before Christmas," that made the rounds at network headquarters—as reported by *Newsday*:

'Twas the night before layoffs
And all through Black Rock
Not a worker was smiling
They all were in shock.
Morale was the lowest
It couldn't be worse
No aspirin, no Band-aids, no CBS nurse.
The staffers were frightened
They all wet their beds
While visions of pink slips
Danced in their heads.
And I in my office
Preparing to leave
Awaiting the slaughter
On this Christmas eve.
When out in the hall
There arose such a clatter
I sprang from my desk
To see what was the matter.
When what to my bloodshot eyes should appear
But a short heartless bald man
Who filled me with fear
With a maniacal grin
As cold as a fish
I knew right away
It must be old Tisch.
"No photo, no finance, no doctors, no pages.

Parody

Cut research, cut lunches, cut all of their wages."
At the top of his lungs
We could hear around the hall,
"Now get out and stay out
Don't bother to call."
He handed to me with a sly little smirk
The pink slip which meant I too had no work.
He sprang to his limo and left right on time
And away they all flew from the scene of the crime.
And I heard him exclaim as he drove out of sight,
Merry Christmas to all and turn off the light."

Anonymous

XI

Musical Wit

Comtesse de Bremont
Max Reger
Rosa Ponselle
Leopold Godowsky
Jascha Heifetz
Billy Rose and Igor Stravinsky
Time Study Experts

A letter is the consolation of life.
—*Voltaire*

DEAR WIT

Comtesse de Bremont

When W. S. Gilbert, lyricist for the Gilbert and Sullivan operettas, demanded a preposterous fee for an interview with Comtesse de Bremont, the Comtesse countered with this biting wit:

> The Comtesse de Bremont presents her compliments to Mr. W. S. Gilbert and, in reply to his answer to her request for an interview for St. Paul's in which he states his terms as 20 guineas for that privilege, begs to say that she anticipates the pleasure of writing his obituary for nothing.

Comtesse de Bremont

Max Reger

Irate musician Max Reger once sent this note to a critic who had lambasted one of the composer's favorite works. This necessary-room jibe also has been attributed to Voltaire:

[Sir:]

> I am sitting in the smallest room of my house. I have your review before me. In a moment it will be behind me.

[*Max Reger*]

Rosa Ponselle

After coloratura Lily Pons made her Metropolitan Opera debut, she received this message from the reigning diva, Rosa Ponselle:

> To Lily Pons, who, I am afraid, is going to knock the "elle" out of Ponselle.
>
> *Rosa*

Leopold Godowsky

The late piano virtuoso, Leopold Godowsky, once received a note from a prominent dowager, asking whether her daughter's musical compositions would live as long as the works of the great musicians. Godowsky replied:

> My Dear Madam,
>
> Yes, I think that your daughter's compositions will live long after those of Mozart, Beethoven, and Tschaikowsky have been forgotten—but not before.
>
> Very sincerely yours,
>
> *Leopold Godowsky*

Jascha Heifetz

As he was about to enter the stage at Carnegie Hall, the master violinist, Jascha Heifetz, was handed this note:

Dear Mr. Heifetz:

Today is my husband's birthday. He doesn't like music, but I am bringing him to your concert anyway. Sometime during the program, would you please play "Happy Birthday to You"—I'm sure it would please him.

Mrs. R. F.

Hastily, Heifetz dashed off this note:

My dear Madam:

I'd be delighted to play "Happy Birthday to You" for your husband, but unfortunately I did not bring the music with me.

Jascha Heifetz

Billy Rose and
Igor Stravinsky

Igor Stravinsky composed a ballet for a Broadway musical produced by Billy Rose. After the opening performance, Rose sent this cable to the great musician:

Stravinsky

   Your music great success stop could be sensational if you would authorize Robert Russell Bennett retouch orchestration stop Bennett orchestrates even the works of Cole Porter.

                                                    Rose

Stravinsky cabled back:

Rose

   Satisfied with great success.

                                                    Stravinsky

Time Study Experts

Feeling that a symphony concert they attended lasted too long, a group of British time study experts submitted this analysis to the conductor of the orchestra:

Dear Mr. Conductor:

For considerable periods the four oboe players had nothing to do. The number should be reduced and the work spread more evenly over the whole of the concert, thus eliminating peaks of activity. All of twelve violins were playing identical notes; this seems unnecessary duplication. The staff of this section should be drastically cut. If a larger volume of sound is required, it could be obtained by electronic apparatus.

Much effort was absorbed in the playing of demisemiquavers; this seems to be unnecessary refinement. It is recommended that all notes should be rounded out to the nearest semiquaver. If this were done it would be possible to use trainees and lower grade operatives more extensively.

No useful purpose is served by repeating on the horns a passage which has already been handled by the strings. It is estimated that if all theme repetitions were eliminated the whole concert-time of two hours could be reduced to twenty minutes and there would be no need for an intermission.

Time Study, Ltd.

XII

Whimsical Wit

Horace Walpole
William Cullen Bryant
Robert Louis Stevenson
Lewis Carroll
O. Henry
G. K. Chesterton
Frank N. Wilcox
Arthur Train
Jackie Gleason
Will Rogers
S. J. Perelman
Edward G. Moran and John L. Marion

We lay aside letters never to read them again, and
at last we destroy them out of discretion, and so
LETTERS disappears the most beautiful, the most immediate breath of life, irrecoverably for ourselves and for
others.
—*Goethe*

Horace Walpole

"With a refined gallantry that both flatters and amuses," one of the great letter writers expresses his devotion to the Duchess of Grafton. The Queen, to whom Walpole compares the Duchess, was Charlotte Sophia, royal mate of George III—America's last King:

My dear Duchess,

   With all your favours your Grace has mixed a little unkindness—when I was to answer your letter, you must know I should wish to write of nothing but you—you enjoin me to talk of the Queen . . . To begin then, Madam, she is of the best proportioned height in the world; her person is so exactly formed, that it would please though motionless, and yet she has an air of as much dignity as is compatible with the most amiable softness; her eyes have more fire, her teeth are whiter, her hair is better disposed, her neck—oh! Lord bless me, I forgot—it was the Queen I was to describe—She is nothing of all this; she is as unlike the description I have been giving as—as—as every woman in the world is but one.

Horace Walpole

William Cullen Bryant

William Cullen Bryant, famed for his *Thanatopsis*, informed his mother of a dramatic experience in which he found himself playing the principal role:

Dear Mother:

... Early on the evening of the eleventh day of the present month I was at a neighboring house in this village. Several people of both sexes were assembled in one of the apartments ... At last came in a little elderly gentleman, pale, thin, with a solemn countenance, pleuritic voice, hooked nose, and hollow eyes. It was not long before we were summoned to attend in the apartment where he and the rest of the company were gathered. We went in and took our seats; the little elderly gentleman with the hooked nose prayed, and we all stood up. When he had finished, most of us sat down. The gentleman with the hooked nose then muttered certain cabalistical expressions which I was too much frightened to remember, but I recollect that at the conclusion I was given to understand that I was married to a young lady of the name of Frances Fairchild, whom I perceived standing by my side, and I hope in the course of a few months to have the pleasure of introducing to you as your daughter-in-law ...

Thus the current of destiny carries us all along. None but a madman would swim against the stream, and none but a fool would exert himself to swim with it. The best way is to float quietly with the tide ...

Your affectionate son,

William

Robert Louis Stevenson

Defeated in health but not in spirits, Robert Louis Stevenson offers to trade his sickly body for that of his robust friend, poet and critic Cosmo Monkhouse:

April 24, 1884

My dear Monkhouse,

If you are in love with repose, here is your occasion: change with me. I am too blind to read, hence no reading; I am too weak to walk, hence no walking; I am not allowed to speak, hence no talking; but the great simplification has yet to be named; for if this goes on, I shall soon have nothing to eat—and hence, O Hallelujah! hence no eating.

The offer is a fair one: I have not sold myself to the devil for I could never find him. I am married, but so are you. I sometimes write verses, but so do you! . . .

True, the tenement is falling. Ay, friend, but yours also. Take a larger view; what is a year or two? dust in the balance! 'Tis done, behold you Cosmo Stevenson, and me R. L. Monkhouse. . . .

There is one article I wish to take away with me: my spirits. They suit me. I don't want yours; I like my own; I have had them a long while in bottle. It is my only reservation. —Yours (as you decide),

R. L. *Monkhouse*

Lewis Carroll

Lewis Carroll, shy and retiring, preferred the company of children to adults. His letters to them, in *Alice in Wonderland* style, have delighted both young and old for many years:

Christ Church, Oxford
October 28, 1876

My dearest Gertrude,

You will be sorry, and surprised, and puzzled, to hear what a queer illness I have had ever since you went. I sent for the doctor, and said, "Give me some medicine, for I'm tired." He said, "Nonsense and stuff! You don't want medicine: go to bed!" I said, "No, it isn't the sort of tiredness that wants bed. I'm tired in the face."

He looked a little grave, and said, "Oh, it's your nose that's tired: a person often talks too much when he thinks he nose a great deal." I said, "No, it isn't the nose. Perhaps it's the hair." Then he looked rather grave, and said, "Now I understand: you've been playing too many hairs on the pianoforte." "No, indeed I haven't!" I said . . .

"Well," he said, "it puzzles me very much. Do you think that it's in the lips?" "Of course!" I said. "That's exactly what it is!"

Then he looked very grave indeed and said, "I think you must have been giving too many kisses." "Well," I said, "I did give one kiss to a baby child, a little friend of mine." "Think again," he said, "are you sure it was only one?" I thought again, and said, "Perhaps it was eleven times." Then the doctor said, "You must not give her any more till your lips are quite rested again." "But what am I to do?" I said, "because you see, I owe her a hundred and eighty-two more."

Then he looked so grave that the tears ran down his cheeks, and he said, "You may send them to her in a box."

Then I remembered a little box that I once bought at Dover, and thought I would some day give it to some little girl or other. So I have packed them all in it very carefully. Tell me if they come safe or if any are lost on the way.

Lewis Carroll

O. Henry

The author of stories with surprise endings, William Sydney Porter (O. Henry), was imprisoned in the Ohio State Penitentiary for misappropriating funds. From his cell, he penned these charming lines to his daughter who did not know where he was:

July 8, 1898

Hello, Margaret:

Don't you remember me? I'm a Brownie, and my name is Aldibirontiphostiphornikophokos. If you see a star shoot and say my name seventeen times before it goes out, you will find a diamond ring in the track of the first blue cow's foot you see go down the road in a snowstorm while the red roses are blooming on the tomato vines. Try it some time . . . Well good-bye, I've got to take a ride on a grasshopper. I'll just sign my first letter—

"A."

G. K. Chesterton

Gilbert K. Chesterton, maven of the paradox, sheds his shell of sophistication in announcing an important event to his close friend Mildred Wain:

My dear Mildred:

On rising this morning, I carefully washed my boots in hot water and blacked my face. Then assuming my coat with graceful ease and with the tail in front, I descended to breakfast, where I gaily poured the coffee on the sardines and put my hat on the fire to boil. These activities will give you some idea of my frame of mind. My family, observing me leave the house by way of the chimney, and take the fender with me under one arm, thought I must have something on my mind. So I had.

My friend, I am engaged. I am only telling it at present to my real friends: but there is no doubt about it.

G. K. C.

Frank N. Wilcox

Your editor, when but a few days old, received a miniature suit of work clothes, accompanied by this communication from Frank N. Wilcox, the much admired attorney and man of letters who died only three months after writing this letter:

June 30, 1904

To the most recent Lang,
My dear young Sir:

As you will know when you become better acquainted with me, I was seized upon learning of your arrival, with a desire to send you greeting forthwith, but my condition has prevented my doing that as speedily as I should wish. However, all the prevailing compliments are yours, together with every assurance of my interest, friendship, and best wishes.

I know your father full well. As a gentleman and a shrewd man of affairs I esteem him most highly. He is in every way competent to feed and clothe you. In the dispensations of Providence, however, and according to the principles of the division of labor, the feeding process will doubtless be left to another, and he be confined to the task of clothing you.

This, as I said, he can do amply, but with your permission I wish to assist, too. Your father is apt to be influenced by a pampered pride and admiration, and clothe you in too sumptuous raiment, forgetful of the fact that you must work as he has done. Therefore, I take the liberty of sending you sane and useful garments, mere pants and shirt, but good. They are strong and substantial and made for toil. May you be so, and labor well. It is our earthly portion, and the sweetness of our pleasure.

By coincidence I read this the same day after I had written a similar type of letter to newly born (Nov 5 1991) Stephane Earle Dubois —

DEAR WIT

My heart goes out to you and my hand for all it's worth. Grow, be stalwart and hearty: smile, frown not, and persevere, and as the years roll round, consider as one of those who wishes you *most* well.

Your servant,

Frank N. *Wilcox*

Arthur Train

"Dear Mr. Train," wrote a sixteen-year-old boarding school girl to the author of the Mr. Tutt stories, "I love you . . . I love you . . . please meet me at the corner of Broadway and 42nd Street." Mr. Train replied:

Dear Miss:

I am sorry I cannot keep that date with you next Sunday afternoon on Broadway and Forty-second Street, but at that hour I always take my grandchildren to Central Park. Should you care to change the place of our rendezvous, you can identify me as the stout gentleman with white whiskers pushing a double perambulator, and wearing a daisy in his hat band. Looking forward to meeting you shortly.

Sincerely yours,

Arthur Train

Jackie Gleason

In 1977, Jackie Gleason placed this note and a blanket of roses on the casket of restauranteur Toots Shor:

Dear Toots:

Hold a table for us.

Jackie

Editor's Note: Ten years later, in 1987, Jackie departed to join his friend Toots.

Will Rogers

Even in times of sadness, Will Rogers never lost his sense of whimsy. He once addressed these tragicomic words to a dear, departed friend:

Dear Charley:

I bet you hadn't been up there three days until you had out your pencil and was a drawin' something funny. And I bet you that a whole bunch of those great old joshers was just a waitin' for you to pop in with all the latest ones.

And I bet they are regular fellows when you meet 'em, ain't they? Most big men are.

Well, you will run onto my old Dad up there, Charley, for he was a real cowhand, and I bet he is runnin' a wagon; and you will pop into some well-kept ranchhouse over under some cool shade trees, and you will be asked to dinner, and it will be the best one you ever had in your life. Well, when you are thankin' the women folks you just tell the sweet lookin' little old lady that you knew her boy, back on an outfit you used to rope for, and tell the daughters that you knew their brother, and if you see a cute little rascal runnin' around there with my brand on him, kiss him for me.

Well, can't write any more, Charley, paper's all wet, it must be raining in this old bunkhouse.

From your old friend,

Will

S. J. Perelman

Recently, actress Julie Haydon (*Glass Menagerie*) announced that she had sold a book "containing just love letters to her dog." Not to be outdone, humorist S. J. Perelman rushed to his publisher the billet-doux written to him by his young beagle hound. Comments Perelman, "the felicity of phrase, the emotional maturity which mark these letters would be arresting in a full-grown dog, in a six-months old puppy, they are nothing short of extraordinary."

September 27

Dear Chief:

I'm no doctor, but I'll give you some friendly advice. That shade of purple you've taken to turning recently, every time anything unusual happens, has me worried. One minute you're your usual shark's-belly white, and the next, without any transition, you look like an eggplant. Better watch the old temper, Mac.

For instance, Tuesday night, when you came home from the movies. O.K., somebody had short-circuited the lamps, eaten a hole in the sofa, and strewn kapok all over the floor. It might have been anyone . . . I could have told you that your domestic lost three previous jobs because of her appetite for sofas. Instead, you chased me through the apartment, screaming the most blood-curdling oaths, and flailing around with a broom. Personally, I enjoyed the romp and slept beautifully afterward, even if you did puff like a donkey engine all night long. Don't play beanbag with your arteries, brother, or you'll wind up in a rolling chair at French Lick.

Speaking of health, maybe you'd like to know what kind of starvation diet one member of the family unit is subsisting on. For dinner today, I was fed a moist mash ... I come into the dining room and find you, with your napkin tucked in below your third chin, gorging yourself on pot roast, baked potato, buttered carrots, chocolate cake, and coffee. All it needed to complete the composition was a big platter and an apple in your mouth. . . .

Adoringly,

Flash

Edward G. Moran Jr.
and John L. Marion

In the letters column of the *New York Times* appeared this exchange of letters between neighbors Edward G. Moran Jr. and John L. Marion, whose dog Prince speaks for his master:

Dear John,

I have been very impressed over the past four or five weeks how smart you new dog, Prince, is. "How does Ed know our dog is so smart?" you are asking yourself. Well, I know he is smart because he reads the *New York Times* almost every day. Unfortunately he is reading my *New York Times*, and some days he just tears out what he wants for his scrapbook, but other days he takes the whole paper home to be read by the pool.

I was wondering if you could give Prince a calendar and then I will leave a day-old paper out every night in the hopes that he will take yesterday's paper every day instead of today's. This way he will be only one day behind in his news, but that will still give him a leg up on the other dogs in the neighborhood.

Sincerely yours,

Ed

Neighbor Moran received this reply from the apologetic Prince:

Dear Moran,

Since retrieving your letter, my master has been hounding me to cease my morning strolls in your neighborhood, and I hope that you appreciate the fact that your *New York Timeses* are no longer dog-eared. Obviously, all your news is not fit for Prince!

Your best friend,

Prince

XIII

Presidential Wit

Thomas Jefferson
Abraham Lincoln
Ulysses S. Grant
Grover Cleveland
Theodore Roosevelt
Woodrow Wilson
Herbert Hoover
Philip James Roosevelt and Franklin Delano Roosevelt
Franklin Delano Roosevelt
Harry Truman
Sam Snead to Richard Nixon
James Michener and Lyndon Baines Johnson
John F. Kennedy
Art Buchwald (Lyndon Baines Johnson)

Life would split asunder without letters.
—*Virginia Woolf*

DEAR WIT

Thomas Jefferson

Thomas Jefferson explained to a Baltimore editor why certain phrases were deleted from the original wording of the Declaration of Independence. He then proceeded to give Benjamin Franklin's formula for avoiding such mutilations:

Monticello
December 4, 1818

To Robert Walsh:

When the Declaration of Independence was under the consideration of Congress, there were two or three unlucky expressions in it which gave offense to some members . . .

I was sitting by Doctor Franklin, who perceived that I was not insensible to these mutilations. "I have made it a rule," said he, "whenever in my power, to avoid becoming the draftsman of papers to be reviewed by a public body. I took my lesson from an incident which I will relate to you. When I was a journeyman printer, one of my companions, an apprentice hatter, having served out his time, was about to open shop for himself. His first concern was to have a handsome sign-board, with a proper inscription. He composed it in these words, 'John Thompson, *Hatter, makes and sells hats for ready money*,' with a figure of a hat subjoined; but he thought he would submit it to his friends for their amendments. The first he showed it to thought the word '*Hatter*', tautologous, because followed by the words '*makes hats*,' which show he was a real hatter. It was struck out. The next observed that the word '*makes*' might as well be omitted, because his customers would not care who made the hats. . . . He struck it out. A third said he thought the words *'for ready money'* were useless, as it was not the custom of the place to sell on credit. . . . They were parted with, and the inscription now stood, 'John Thompson *sells hats.*' '*Sells hats!*' says his next friend: 'why nobody will expect you to give them away; what then is the use of that word?' It was stricken out, and '*hats*' followed it, the rather as there was one painted on the board. So the inscription was reduced ultimately to 'John Thompson,' with the figure of a hat subjoined."

Th. *Jefferson*

Abraham Lincoln

Despite the contrariness of some members of his cabinet, particularly Secretary of the Treasury, Samuel P. Chase, Abraham Lincoln's sense of humor never deserted him. When the collector of the port of New York sent a job seeker to Lincoln the President replied:

Simeon Draper, Esqu.
Collector of the Port of New York

My dear Sir:—

Your friend called on me when he arrived and presented your letter. As I have no influence with this administration, I sent him to Chase. Chase told him to go to the devil, and he came back to me.

Yours truly,

A. *Lincoln*

Ulysses S. Grant

Ulysses S. Grant, conquering hero of the Civil War, was ever a man of action. In his last days, as death soon was to end his suffering, Grant handed this note to his doctor:

Dear Doctor,

The fact is that I think I am a verb instead of a personal pronoun. A verb is anything that signifies to be; or to do; or to suffer. I signify all three.

U. S. *Grant*

Grover Cleveland

A citizen wrote Grover Cleveland asking whether Mrs. Cleveland had franking privileges to mail letters free of postage. The president, who completed two full terms in office, explained why he was grateful that his first lady did not qualify:

Dear Sir,

I have no postal frank, nor does Mrs. Cleveland. I believe franks do not go to the wives of the Presidents until they become widows, and I am not anxious to hasten that day.

Grover Cleveland

Theodore Roosevelt

Theodore Roosevelt, one-time Rough Rider, rides rough shod over a member of his Progressive party—later known as the "Bull Moose" party on which ticket TR again ran for president, but was defeated by Woodrow Wilson:

Sir:

When I spoke of the Progressive party as having a lunatic fringe, I specifically had you in mind. On the supposition that you are of entire sound mind, I should be obliged to say that you are absolutely dishonorable and untruthful. I prefer to accept the former alternative.

Yours truly . . .

Theodore Roosevelt

Woodrow Wilson

When Woodrow Wilson was courting his First-Lady-to-be, he sent her a corsage with this supreme compliment. Edith Galt Wilson was later to be called "the first woman president," for attending to Wilson's duties when he lay helplessly ill.

> You are the only woman I know who can wear an orchid. Generally it is the orchid that wears the woman.   COMPLIM
>
> *Woodrow*

Herbert Hoover

Judy, a junior high school student assigned a social study of great men of this century, chose our thirteenth president. "Could you," she wrote Herbert Hoover, "send me some information on your life?" The president replied:

Dear Judy:

I am sending you some information on my life. The printed information which I have on hand is either by friends who overstate my virtues, or by opponents who seem oblivious to them. I send you one of the evaluations of a friend.

Herbert Hoover

Philip James Roosevelt and
Franklin Delano Roosevelt

After-dinner speakers evoked many a chuckle in the early days of Franklin Roosevelt's administration by quoting this apocryphal correspondence between Philip James Roosevelt and his cousin Franklin:

Dear Cousin Franklin:

As you know, I am trustee of the estate left you by your father. It is very difficult to invest money safely in these times. I should be much obliged if you would answer the following questions so that I can administer the estate to your best advantage as beneficiary: Do you intend further to devalue the dollar? Do you intend to continue government spending to the point where serious inflation will follow? What do you intend to do about silver?

Phil

Dear Cousin Phil:

You're the trustee.

Franklin

Dear Cousin Franklin:

I have put all the funds, formerly invested in various securities, into government bonds.
Now you're the trustee.

Phil

DEAR WIT

Franklin Delano Roosevelt

Robert Sherwood, playwright and biographer of Franklin Delano Roosevelt, uncovered some unpublished correspondence between FDR and William Allen White, the "Sage of Emporia," Kansas. This brief note accompanied a photo of FDR in his favorite seersucker suit:

Dear Bill:

Here is the seersucker picture, duly inscribed by the sucker to the seer.

F. D. R.

Harry Truman

President Harry Truman once received a letter from Mississippian Hugh C. Ellis, saying that he had a bet he could get a personally autographed photo of the president. "Give 'em hell" Harry replied with this unsigned letter:

December 6, 1954

Dear Mr. Ellis:

I am not going to treat you as President Coolidge treated the young lady who sat by him at dinner. She tried all evening to get him into a conversation and all she could get was—yes or no or a grunt. She finally told him that she had made a bet that she could get him to say more than three words during the dinner. He merely said to her—"You lose."

Sincerely yours,

(*Unsigned*)

Sam Snead to
Richard Nixon

Golf pro Sam Snead dared to offer President Nixon advice on how to keep from being too far to the left or right:

Dear Mr. President:

I'm aware that the White House is already swarming with advisors and that your administration can probably get along fine without any coaching from a Virginia hillbilly named Sam Snead. But, sir, *This Week* magazine recently called my attention to some photographs of your recent golf swing and—well—I just feel it's my patriotic duty to speak out on a matter of grave importance to the executive branch of our government. . . .

I recently read a column by a political analyst who said, "President Nixon is a little to the right of center." I guess that's a pretty good position, for politics. But in golf, it's a pro's duty to see that the President does not end up so far both to the right *and* left of center that he'll find himself out-of-bounds most of the time.

I once had a pivotal discussion on a related subject with President Eisenhower when he invited me to comment one day on some problems that were bothering his administration.

"They keep telling me to turn, turn, turn my body if I want more distance off the tee," Ike said as he took a practice swing. "What do you think?"

"If you want more distance, Mr. President," I replied, "don't stand so straight. You must stick your butt out."

Saying that to the President of the United States was one of the hardest things I've ever had to do. Some of the bodyguards winced. But Ike didn't bat an eyelash.

"I could have sworn it was stuck out pretty far already," he said.

"Not enough, sir," I gulped.

I can only trust, Mr. Nixon, that you will accept my unsolicited advice in the spirit with which I offer it. I'm sure that for the good of the game, respect for you, and love of his country, every pro in the land stands personally ready to meet you on the practice range and make sure that four years from now you'll not be right or left of center—but straight down the middle.

Sincerely yours,

Sam Snead

James Michener and
Lyndon Baines Johnson

Best-selling author James Michener once declined an invitation to a dinner with President Lyndon Johnson in the White House, for a very special reason:

Dear Mr. President,

> I received your invitation three days after I had agreed to speak a few words at a dinner honoring the wonderful high school teacher who taught me how to write. I know you will not miss me at your dinner, but she might at hers.

James Michener

Fully understanding, President Johnson commented as follows:

[Dear Michener,]

> . . . In his lifetime a man lives under 15 or 16 presidents, but a really fine teacher comes into his life but rarely.

Lyndon Johnson

John F. Kennedy

In 1960, a California writer reminded John F. Kennedy of the ominous coincidence that since 1840 every U.S. president elected in a year ending in a zero had died in office. William Henry Harrison (1840) died of pneumonia only one month after his inauguration; Warren G. Harding (1920) succumbed to a fatal ailment. Franklin Roosevelt (1940) died of a stroke. Lincoln (1860), Garfield (1880), and McKinely (1900) were all assassinated. Not knowing his fate, JFK responded with his usual sense of humor:

Dear Mr. Squires:

I feel that the future will have to answer this for itself both as to my aspirations and my fate should I have the privilege of occupying the White House. I dare say, should anyone take this phenomenon to heart, anyone, that is, who aspires to change his address to 1600 Pennsylvania Avenue ... most probably the landlord would be left from 1960–64 with a "For Rent" sign hanging on the gatehouse door.

Sincerely,

John F. Kennedy

Art Buchwald (Lyndon Baines Johnson)

In his amusing, whimsical style, Art Buchwald composed this note from Lyndon Johnson, which newly elected President Richard Nixon and his First Lady might have found pinned to the door of the White House when they moved in:

Dear Dick and Pat,

The key is under the doormat and you can have all the food that's left in the ice box . . .

Garbage goes out Friday, trash on Monday, but don't mix the two or there is a $25 fine. For example, don't throw out your budget messages with your news secretary's briefing transcripts.

The appliances are all in pretty good shape, though it gets hot in the kitchen every once in a while. You can blame Harry Truman for that. He knew about the problem, but every time someone wanted to do something about it, he said, "If you can't stand the heat, get out of the kitchen."

Lady Bird's left a list of handymen to call if you need anything repaired. If you call the plumber and tell him you're the President of the United States, he'll be over within 48 hours . . .

I guess that's pretty much it. I think you'll like the house. It has a certain something to it that's hard to explain.

The only advice I have is don't get too attached to the place. The landlords are pretty fickle people, and no matter what you do for them, if they take a dislike to you they'll kick you out . . .

Sincerely,

Lyndon

XIV

Historic Wit

King Archidamus
Third Earl of Pembroke
Thornton Wilder (Julius Caesar)
Benjamin Franklin
Patrick Henry
Sir Charles Napier
Duke of Wellington
Viscount Palmerston
Thomas B. Reed
Jacob Riis
Maria Taft
Alexander Woollcott
Wit of the Irish
Wernher von Braun
Jessie Helms and John Tower

A historian is a person who gets to read other people's mail.
　　—*Anonymous*

King Archidamus

After his victorious conquest of Greece, Philip of Macedon received this incisive note from the King of Sparta. Possibly it was in anticipation of Ralph Waldo Emerson's oft quoted saying, "An institution is the lengthened shadow of a man":

Philip of Macedon:

If you measure your shadow, you will find it no greater than before the victory.

Archidamus
King of Sparta

Third Earl of Pembroke

Oliver Cromwell became ruler of the British Empire after sanctioning the beheading of Charles I. One of Cromwell's detractors, the Third Earl of Pembroke, to whom Shakespeare's *First Folio* was dedicated, addressed this note to posterity in his last will and testament:

I give to Lieutenant-General Cromwell one of my words, that which he must want, seeing that he hath never kept any of his own.

Earl of Pembroke

Thornton Wilder
(Julius Caesar)

A balding Caesar reveals his human side in this letter to "the most beautiful woman in the world." (As wittily recontructed by Thornton Wilder in *The Ides of March*.)

October
45 B.C.

Caesar to Cleopatra:

Oh, yes. I obey the Queen of Egypt. I do everything she tells me to do.

The top of my head has been purple all day.

Visitor after visitor has looked at me with horror, but no one has asked me what was the matter with me. That is what it is to be a Dictator; no one asks him a question about himself. I could hop on one foot from here to Ostia and back and no one would mention it—*to me*.

At last a cleaning woman came in to wash the floor. She said, "Oh, divine Caesar, what is the matter with your head?"

"Little mother," I said, "the greatest woman in the world, the most beautiful woman in the world, the wisest woman in the world said that baldness is cured by rubbing the head with a salve made of honey, juniper berries, and wormwood. She ordered me to apply it and I obey her in everything."

"Divine Caesar," she replied, "I am not great nor beautiful nor wise, but this one thing I know: a man can have either hair or brains, but he can't have both. You're quite beautiful enough as you are, sir; and since the Immortal Gods gave you good sense, I think they didn't mean for you to have curls."

I am thinking of making that woman a Senator.

Caius Julius Caesar

DEAR WIT

Benjamin Franklin

When Benjamin Franklin invited Edward Gibbon to dinner, the author of *The Decline and Fall of the Roman Empire* declined, saying that while he respected Franklin as a philosopher, he could not visit anyone revolting against the King. Wily, old Ben replied:

Dear Mr. Gibbon,

I have such a high regard for you as a historian that if you would consider the decline and fall of the British Empire as a subject, I would be very happy to furnish you with some relevant materials.

B. *Franklin*

Patrick Henry

An unnamed government official once wrote Patrick Henry, demanding satisfaction for being called a "bobtail politician." The fiery patriot, in no mood for a duel, sent this reply:

Sir:

I do not recollect having called you a "bobtail" politician at any time, but think it probable I have. Not recollecting the time or occasion, I can't say what I did mean, but if you will tell me what you think I meant, I will say whether you are correct or not.

Very respectfully,

Patrick Henry

Sir Charles Napier

Sir Charles Napier was a distinguished British commander. After the old province of Sind in Pakistan was captured in 1840, the British Foreign Office received this one-word message, from the conquering general:

Peccavi

Sir Charles Napier

Editor's Note: Translated it means: "I have sinned."

Duke of Wellington

After defeating Napoleon at Waterloo, the Duke of Wellington signed off with this uncomplimentary close in a searing letter to one of his officers:

I have the honor to be, sir, your humble and obedient servant (which you know damn well I am not).

Wellington

Viscount Palmerston

Viscount Palmerston, British Foreign Minister, advises Queen Victoria on the proprieties of correspondence with the Sovereign of Lucca, an independent Italian state:

Stanhope Street,
5th March 1839

[Your Majesty]

Viscount Palmerston presents his humble duty to your Majesty . . . and . . . begs to state that he has reason to believe . . . that the Duke of Lucca has a notion that sovereign Princes who have had the honour of dining with your Majesty, have been invited by note and not by card. If that should be so, and if your Majesty should invite the Duke of Lucca to dine at the Palace before his departure, perhaps the invitation might be made by note, instead of by card, as it was when the Duke last dined at the Palace. Your Majesty may think this a small matter, but the Duke is a small Sovereign.

Palmerston

Thomas B. Reed

Gar Reed, dictatorial Speaker of the House, was called "Tsar Reed." One of his opponents sent him a letter of denunciation ending with the words, "I would rather be right than Speaker of the House." The sharp-witted Reed replied:

My dear Sir:

You need have no fear. You will never be either.

Thomas B. Reed

ʃ

Jacob Riis

Roger William Riis, son of social reformer Jacob Riis, reports his father once received a letter from a woman who had always admired Theodore Roosevelt, but she heard that when storming San Juan Hill, the colonel had said "Damn." If it were true, she would be compelled to change her opinion, and would Mr. Riis please let her know. He did:

Dear Madam:

RIPOSTE

I do not know whether Colonel Roosevelt said "Damn" when he went up San Juan Hill, but I know I did when I read your letter.

Yours truly,

Jacob Riis

Maria Taft

When Maria, the daughter of William Howard Taft III, was a shy young schoolgirl she was asked by her teacher for a brief family history. This is what Maria wrote:

My great-grandfather was President of the United States. My grandfather was Senator from Ohio. My father is Ambassador to Ireland. I am a Brownie.

Child-

irony
(accidental or deliberately)   Maria

Alexander Woollcott

Alexander Woollcott once wrote to his niece, Joan, who was trying to trace the Woollcott ancestry to American Revolutionary General Joseph Warren. Woollcott gives undeniable reasons why his niece is on the wrong trail:

Bomoseen, Vermont

Dear Joan,

Is it the Daughters of the American Revolution you are trying to get into? Even though I suspect you of intentions to bore from within I must pass on a word of warning about General Warren. He was a lively and public-spirited medico who was appointed general overnight, arrayed himself gaudily to suit that rank, made himself conspicuous on a parapet at Bunker Hill, and was therefore popped off in the first ten minutes of the battle. However, it is not because he was a bad general that you should avoid claiming descent from him. It is because he was a bachelor.

Your descent is in the direct line from his brother, Stephen, who was properly married all right and to whom, as a wedding gift, Joseph Warren presented the bedroom furniture of which the chest of drawers in due time came to me. I gave it to your father because he seemed more likely to abound in descendants. Your great-great-grandmother was Lydia Warren. . . .

A. *Woollcott*

Wit of the Irish

Humorist Sam Levenson revealed this exchange between a Northern Irish farm wife and her IRA revolutionist husband whose letters from a British prison had to pass the censor:

Dear Mike:

The fates are against us. There is no one left to plow the potato field. Without potatoes we will starve this winter. Whatever shall I do?

Lovingly,

Bridget

Dear Bridget:

Sorry to hear things are going so badly with you. But whatever you do, don't plow up the potato field . . . the ammunition is buried there!

Affectionately,

Mike

Dear Mike:

The bleedin' British must have read your last letter. They came yesterday and plowed up the whole potato field looking for the ammunition.

Lovingly,

Bridget

Dear Bridget:

Now plant the potatoes!

Affectionately,

Mike

Wernher von Braun

Jim Bishop, author of *A Day In The Life of President Kennedy*, organized a Distinguished Duffers Golf Tournament and sent invitations to celebrities who shoot over 100. One of his replies came from Wernher von Braun, before he directed the first successful Gemini shot.

Dear Mr. Bishop:

The only ball I am seriously intent on hitting is one that shows up every evening in the east, and I do not expect to hit it until 1969.

I had considered volunteering as scorekeeper, but over the years I have gotten into the habit of counting backward— 10, 9, 8, 7—and this would lift all the participants out of the duffer class.

Wernher von Braun

Jessie Helms and John Tower

Promoting his home state of North Carolina, Senator Jesse Helms once sent each of his colleagues a box of home-grown pickles, with this note:

Dear Colleague,

> Peter Piper, no matter how many pecks of pickled pepper he might have picked, was a pathetically pooped picker compared to North Carolina's achievement in the pickle business.

Jessie Helms

Briefest and wittiest of the many thank-you letters Helms received was this quickie from Senator John Tower, whose challenged ethics lost his appointment to Secretary of Defense:

Dear Helms,

> I was pickled tink.

Tower

X V

Stage and Screen Wit

Richard Brinsley Sheridan
Sarah Bernhardt
Oscar Wilde
Alexander Woollcott
Moss Hart
Alexander Pantages
W. C. Fields
George S. Kaufman
James Thurber
Humphrey Bogart
W. S. Gilbert
Sir John Gielgud
James Stewart
Cary Grant

There are certain people whom one almost feels inclined to urge to hurry up and die so that their letters can be published.
—*Christopher Morley*

Richard Brinsley Sheridan

When an admiring lady fan wrote to ask Richard Brinsley Sheridan the essential difference between man and woman, the famous British playwright replied:

Dear Madam,

I cannot conceive.

Sincerely yours,

Richard Brinsley Sheridan

} ST
} WORD PLAY

Sarah Bernhardt

Following an accident in which she lost a leg, the celebrated French actress received this cable:

We offer you 100,000 dollars to exhibit your leg at our Exposition in Buffalo.

Pan American

DR
ST

Jovial as usual, the undaunted Bernhardt cabled back:

Which one?

Sarah Bernhardt

Oscar Wilde

After a drama critic had unmercifully panned one of his plays and then heaped insult upon injury by referring to him as "John," Oscar Wilde addressed this letter to the editor:

Dear Sir:

John is an admirable name. It was the name of the most charming of all the disciples, the one who did not write the Fourth Gospel. It was the name of the most perfect of all the English poets of this century, as it was of the greatest English poet of all the centuries. Popes and princes, wicked or wonderful, have been called John. John has been the name of several eminent journalists and criminals. But John is not amongst the many delightful names (they included, besides Oscar, Fingal O'Flahertie Wills) given to me at my baptism. So kindly let me correct the statement made by your reckless dramatic critic in his last and unavailing attack on my play.

The attempt he makes to falsify one of the most important facts in the history of the arts must be checked at once.

Oscar Wilde

Editor's Note: The original autograph of this letter is in the Frances and H. Jack Lang collection at Case Western Reserve University.

Alexander Woollcott

After seeing George S. Kaufman and Moss Hart's *The Man Who Came to Dinner*, a prudish friend sent this letter to Alexander Woollcott:

Dear Alec:

I saw you and your play yesterday and enjoyed both thoroughly except for three unnecessary "G__ d____'s" and a half dozen unnecessarily vulgar "wisecracks." If these were deleted, *The Man Who Came to Dinner* would be a rollicking good comedy which I would be glad to recommend to all of my friends without qualification . . .

T. D. *Martin*

The witty drama critic sent this reply:

My dear Martin:

This is to acknowledge your letter of March sixth, which really shocked me.

When you speak of "three unnecessary G__ d____'s" you imply that there is such a thing as a *necessary* G__ d____. This, of course, is nonsense. A G__ d____ is never a necessity. It is always a luxury.

Yours very sincerely,

Alexander Woollcott

Moss Hart

Playwright Moss Hart, who collaborated with George S. Kaufman on many stage hits, tells Bennett Cerf what he might expect if "The Klobber Method" of bringing up children is applied in his household:

Dear Bennett:

Do you remember, one lovely starlit evening on the desert a few weeks ago, our discussing at some length and with a good deal of parental acrimony, the proper method of bringing up children? That usually discerning and extremely wise lady, your wife, disagreed violently and somewhat haughtily, I thought, at the method we use in our house, but I thought you showed unusual interest in our experiment and silently longed to apply it yourself, so I pass it along to you and to any other frantic and harassed parents who, like ourselves, were damn near ready for the booby hatch until The Klobber Method came into our home.

The Klobber Method was discovered, or rather invented, by Ernest J. Klobber, a Viennese psychiatrist who, at the time of the discovery of the method which was to bear his name, was a staunch believer in the modern and accepted formula for rearing children. Give them a reason for everything—watch out for traumas—plenty of love and security—and never a harsh word. So great an exponent of this formula was Professor Klobber that, at the time of his discovery, the Professor, who has six children of his own, was about to be carted off to a sanitarium in a state of complete nervous collapse; a condition any modern parent will understand at once.

As the stretcher was being carried out of the house, one of the children aimed a kick at it which, with unerring childlike aim, landed exactly where it was meant to land. The Professor, though thoroughly used to being kicked by his children, was under mild sedation at the time, and it may have been this that caused a curious reflex action on the Professor's part. Bringing his arm up from the stretcher, he brought his hand down with a good sharp crack on the child's head. There was an anguished howl from the child—first time in its life no reason had been given for an action—but the effect on the Professor was startling. He leaped up from the stretcher and gave each of the other five kiddies in turn a good smart crack over the head—a Klobber, as he afterward termed it—and never went near the sanitarium.

Instead, in suddenly excellent spirits and health, he began to develop the Klobber Method. No reason was given for anything. "No" meant "no" and "yes" meant "yes," and trauma or no trauma, at the first hint of an argument the children got a Klobber, and life, for the Professor and his good wife, was livable for the first time since the patter of little feet had thundered through the house . . .

The charm of the method, my dear Bennett, is its utter simplicity. In place of long hours of dreary explanation that Daddy cannot work if Junior bangs on the radiator, and if Daddy cannot work and make money, how will we go to the circus; in place of that tortured quiet between husband and wife in the long night hours as to which one warped the childish id by refusing to allow the hot-foot to be applied to Uncle Robert; in place of all that just "Klobber!" and serenity reigns. It is the greatest invention since the wheel, my dear fellow, and as your wife seems to object to it, try it on her first instead of the children and let me know the results . . .

Ever yours,

Moss Hart

Alexander Pantages

Salt Lake City was one of the most lucrative links in the chain of vaudeville houses operated by Alexander Pantages. When the shrewd theater magnate offered a popular troupe a contract that did not include Salt Lake, the following telegrams were quickly exchanged:

ALEXANDER PANTAGES
SALT LAKE CITY, UTAH

> EITHER PLAY US SALT LAKE OR COUNT US OUT.

> > THE BIG CITY FOUR

THE BIG CITY FOUR
NEW YORK, N.Y.

> ONE TWO THREE FOUR FIVE
> > SIX SEVEN EIGHT NINE TEN.

> > ALEXANDER PANTAGES

W. C. Fields

Free-lance writer Mary Ann Frey, engaged in writing an article on the thousands of gloves lost by women every year, came across this letter written by bulbous-nosed W. C. Fields to the manager of a Broadway theater:

Dear Sir:

I am attending the performance at your theater on the eve of September 24. I have seats G-1 and G-2. The reason I am sending you this notification is that I will be accompanied by my wife who will lose a pair of gray suede gloves.

W. C. *Fields*

George S. Kaufman

Seeing Rex Harrison quoted in an advertisement saying, "A martini is like a play . . . it can be terribly good or terribly poor," George S. Kaufman playfully addressed this open letter to the star of "My Fair Lady":

Well, Rex, old boy,

Let's bat this thing around for a couple of minutes . . .

So you . . . said that a martini was like a play. Now as I understand it, a martini has an olive in it. Is this true of a play? Of course, it could have Olive Deering in it, or Olive Wyndham, or Olive Reeves Smith, but how often does that happen? It could even have Olivier in it, but let's not try to get funny. The dramatic critics—anyhow, the good ones—don't like jokes this season. This brings me to the fact that when you bring a martini to New York, the boys don't dream of criticizing it. They just drink it.

Or let's say you're opening a martini in Wilmington, just for a try-out. Do you call up Moss Hart and ask him to come down and take a swig at it, just to see what he thinks? I know Mr. Hart pretty well, and I don't think he wants to come down to Wilmington and sit up all night in a hotel bedroom—not over one martini, anyhow.

Incidentally, I notice from the photograph in the advertisement that your martini doesn't have an olive in it at all—it has a twist of lemon peel in it. This gives Mr. Hart an out on that trip to Wilmington—he suggests that you try twisting the lemon peel to the left instead of the right, and see how that works.

Mind you, I don't really blame you for saying that a martini is like a play, because you certainly know a lot about plays. You just don't know anything about martinis.

George S. Kaufman

James Thurber

When Samuel Goldwyn produced James Thurber's *Life of Walter Mitty*, he sent a copy of the movie script to Thurber. Becoming almost profane when he saw how his story had been mutilated, Thurber wrote Goldwyn a long letter which ended as follows:

Dear Sirs,

... he [Goldwyn] told me the first sixty pages were all right and asked me not to read the last 100 pages, which he said were too "blood and thirsty."

I read the entire script, of course, and was horror and struck.

James Thurber

Humphrey Bogart

Time magazine once ran a department of Current & Choice of the best movies and their casts. When *Time* omitted the name of Lauren Bacall in listing *Key Largo*, the editor received this friendly protest from Humphrey Bogart:

Dear Sir:

It has come to my attention that in your Current & Choice section, Lauren Bacall has consistently been left out of the cast of *Key Largo*.

Inasmuch as there are those of us in Hollywood, Miss Bacall among them, who would rather make Current & Choice than win an Academy Award or make Men of Distinction, won't you please include her in the cast of *Key Largo* in Current & Choice just once, as she is my wife and I have to live with her. Miss Bacall is extremely tired of being labeled *et al*.

Humphrey Bogart

W. S. Gilbert

W. S. Gilbert was the librettist of HMS P*inafore* and other Gilbert and Sullivan Savoyard light operas. After hearing Sir Herbert Beerbohm Tree read *Hamlet*, Gilbert sent this searing comment to an unidentified friend:

[Dear Friend,]

Do you know how they are going to decide the Shakespeare–Bacon dispute? They are going to dig up Shakespeare and dig up Bacon; they are going to set their coffins side by side, and they are going to get Tree to recite *Hamlet* to them. And the one who turns in his coffin will be the author of the play.

W. S. *Gilbert*

Sir John Gielgud

Stage star John Gielgud, grand nephew of Ellen Terry, was noted for his fine performances. In great demand for dinner parties, Gielgud sent this reply to one invitation:

Sir:

Sorry, can't attend your party. Gielgud doesn't fielgud.

JG

James Stewart

Threatened with a suit, George Burns's attorney suggested that George line up some character witnesses. One of them, James Stewart, struggled to comply, in his usual halting style:

Dear George—

I . . . I . . . uh . . . I . . . uh just got this call from your . . . lawyer . . . asking me to write a . . . write a . . . character . . . reference for you.

Well, George, I've . . . uh . . . I've . . . uh . . . known you a good long time. I knew Gracie, too, but that's not what this is about, is it . . .

Anyway, I'd . . . uh . . . I'd . . . uh . . . be happy to . . . write you a . . . uh . . . letter stating whatever it is your lawyer called about. Just have . . . have—Oh, forget it. By the time I get through with this, the trial will be over.

James Stewart

Editor's Note: Mr. Stewart has given his permission to use this letter, with the note that it was actually written by one of his writers.

Cary Grant

An anonymous magazine editor cabled Cary Grant's Hollywood agent:

HOW OLD CARY GRANT?

Mr. Grant answered the cable himself:

OLD CARY GRANT FINE. HOW YOU?

Cary Grant

XVI

TV *and* Radio Wit

Groucho Marx
Ben Bernie and Walter Winchell
Garry Moore
Gabe Dype
Dolly Parton

Man has always been interested in the writing of other persons, perhaps because preserving a piece of their writing is a way of preserving a bit of the persons themselves.

—*Edmund Berkeley, Jr.*

Groucho Marx

When *Variety*, the show magazine, suggested that the Marx brothers could earn twenty thousand or more a week if they would perform together, Groucho wrote the editor:

Dear Sir:

> Apparently you are under the impression that the only thing that matters in this world is money. That is quite true.

> *Groucho Marx*

Ben Bernie and Walter Winchell

After Walter Winchell made his first radio broadcast with musical accompaniment, Ben Bernie, performing in Chicago, sent him this wire:

> You were wonderful stop I have an offer here for you stop five thousand a week for you and the band stop seven thousand for band without you.

> *Ben*

Winchell wired back from New York:

> Dear Mousetro didn't know you were in Chicago stop thought I saw you get out of an empty taxicab in front of the Lamb's Club here.

> *Walter*

Garry Moore

When TV performer Garry Moore received crackpot letters viciously attacking him, he used this standard reply:

Dear Sir:

The enclosed letter arrived on my desk a few days ago. I am sending it to you in the belief that as a responsible citizen you should know that some idiot is sending out letters over your signature.

Cordially,

Garry Moore

Gabe Dype

Hearing that Charles Knepper had been elected vice president of Lang, Fisher & Stashower advertising agency, TV executive Gabe Dype sent him congratulations, tempered with more than a modicum of friendly sarcasm:

BLAIR TELEVISION
Detroit, Michigan

Dear Charlie:

Sincerest congratulations to you on your election as a vice president ... I am delighted for you, and this is well deserved recognition. You've earned every bit of it!

Just to minimize the chances of an overblossoming of your ego as a result of the veep stripe, I want to call your attention to the fact that you are now in the company of other famous vice presidents, including:

Aaron Burr (1801–1805)
Served under Thomas Jefferson, was indicted for murder, and later for treason.

John Breckinridge (1857–1861)
President Buchanan's vice president. Became a Confederate general, refused to surrender, and became a pirate.

Schulyer Colfax (1869–1873)
He suffered disgrace in the Credit Mobilier Scandals, while serving as vice president to U. S. Grant.

Richard Johnson (1837–1841)
Vice president under Martin Van Buren, he left office in mid-term to take care of his saloon in Kentucky.

Best wishes for your continued success!

Kindest personal regards,

Gabe

Dolly Parton

After her tennis shirt slipped down, leaving her topless in front of a shocked Wimbledon audience, an embarrassed Linda Siegel received this consoling note from country-western entertainer Dolly Parton:

Dear Linda Siegel,

I know how you must be feeling. I am a singer-songwriter, but I have to grin and bear all the other things that go with the job. In your case, please remember, handle it with humor. Grin when you bare it—it's the only way.

Dolly Parton

XVII

Tradesmen's Wit

English Quaker
Mary R.
Billy Rose
Irvin Cobb
Fish Friers
John Steinbeck
Al Cooper
Albert S. Kaloa, Jr., and Keith Funston
Stanley Marcus
Los Alamos Laboratories
Necci Sales Manager
Buttery Words
William Safire
John D. Yeck
Hotel Manager
Anson H. Beard and Steve Collins
Maron Simon

FIG)Correspondences are like small clothes before the
invention of suspenders: it is impossible to keep
them up.
—*Sydney Smith*

English Quaker

Found among some old papers was this quaint note addressed by a Quaker sending his pocket clock to his watchmaker for repair.

From Gunnerside, Richmond,
Yorkshire (England)

To my Watchmaker,

I herewith send Thee my pocket clock, which greatly standeth in need of Thy friendly correction. The last time he was at Thy friendly school he was no ways reformed, nor in the least benefited thereby, for I perceive by the Index of his Mind that he is a Liar, and the Truth is not in him. His motions are wavering and irregular. His impulses are sometimes very quick, which betokeneth not an even Temper. At other times he waxeth sluggish, not withstanding . . .

Hence I am induced to believe he is not right in the inward man. Examine him, I beseech Thee, thoroughly, that Thou mayest, by being well acquainted with His inward Frame and Disposition, draw Him from the error of His ways and show Him the Path wherein He should go. . . .

G. Johnson

Mary R.

Asked why she was leaving her position, a stenographer explained in her letter of resignation:

Dear Boss,

My reason for quitting will soon be apparent—and so will

Mary R.

I.
WORD
PLAY

Billy Rose

Showman Billy Rose, one of the cleverest of letter writers, tells Quentin Reynolds the hilarious tale of how buying a gift for his wife, Eleanor, led to a chain reaction:

Dear Quent,

I think you're in trouble—serious trouble. And I'll tell you why.

A few weeks ago I was browsing around one of these antique shops which specialize in Larceny and Old Lace. In a tray of whatchamacallits, I came across a brass mermaid which I thought might look good on one of Eleanor's handbags.

When I gave it to her, Eleanor said, "It's just what I've always wanted. What is it?"

"It's a whatchamacallit," I said.

"It's about time you called off your buyer's strike," said my wife. "Now all I need is a handbag to put it on."

"But you have a handbag," I said. "Several of them."

"None of them is right for it," said Eleanor firmly.

The following evening when we went to the movies, Eleanor was toting one of her old pocketbooks. I asked how come. "My new hat won't be ready for a few days," she said. *FASHION*

I thought I understood. "You mean you ordered a hat to match the handbag which you bought to match the mermaid," I said.

"Not exactly," said Eleanor. "The hat is to match the new suit. My other suit clashed with the new shoes."

"Let's begin at the beginning," I said. "I bought you a whatchamacallit."

"So I bought a bag to put it on," said Eleanor. "Naturally, I had to get shoes to go with the bag. You always match handbags with shoes."

"I do?" I inquired, "You know, I hate to think what would happen to me if you ever decided I clashed with your ensemble."

I gave my wife a little lecture on economy. When I told her how much theater business was off, Eleanor was impressed. The upshot of our talk was that I promised not to take so many taxis.

Next evening when I got home, Eleanor flashed her No. 1 smile. For dessert we had chocolate profiterole. "Let's stay home tonight," she said. "We'll light a fire and listen to the radio."

"What are you after now?" I asked.

Eleanor grinned. "A little fur around my neck to match the new suit. I just want to show the girls how generous my husband is."

Easter morning Eleanor dolled up like the girl in Irving Berlin's *Easter Parade*. Her handbag matched her shoes. Shoes matched gloves. Gloves matched hat. Hat matched blouse. Blouse matched suit. Suit matched fur piece—and the fur piece matched what it cost to police Bowling Green, Kentucky.

But as we strolled up Fifth Avenue I got the feeling that something was missing. "What happened to the brass whatchamacallit on your handbag?" I asked her.

"Oh that," she said, "I had to take if off. It clashed with these earrings."

I suppose, my dear Quent, you're wondering why I bore you with this melancholy recital. Well, today I asked Eleanor for the brass mermaid—thought it might make an interesting paperweight for my desk. Eleanor told me she had given the whatchamacallit to your wife, Ginny.

That's all, brother!

Billy Rose

Irvin Cobb

Newspaper editors might not recommend this application letter as a model for aspiring young job-seekers, but it worked for twenty-seven-year-old Irvin S. Cobb after all other methods had failed.

Editor
New York Post
New York, N.Y.

Sir:

This is positively your last chance. I have grown weary of studying the wallpaper design in your anteroom. A modest appreciation of my own worth forbids me doing business with your head office boy any longer. Unless you grab me right away, I will go elsewhere and leave your paper flat on its back right here in the middle of a hard summer, and your whole life hereafter will be one vast surging regret. The line forms on the right; applications considered in the order in which they are received; triflers and professional flirts save stamps. Write, wire, or call at the above address.

Irvin Cobb

JOB APPLICATION

Fish Friers

When Blackpool, England was host to two national conventions, the British Fish Friers Union wired the British Journalists Union as follows:

FRATERNAL GREETINGS TO
THE NATIONAL UNION OF JOURNALISTS
FROM THE NATIONAL UNION OF FISH FRIERS!
OUR WORK IS WRAPPED UP IN YOURS.

N.U.F.F.

John Steinbeck

John Steinbeck was a prolific writer of superb letters. "It was his way of warming up"—the way he "got the juices flowing." They were flowing well in this letter telling his young writer friend George Albee of his wife Carol's hilarious experiences bargaining in Mexican marketplaces:

[Mexico]
[1935]

Dear George:

    . . . Carol is having a marvelous time. The people like her and she them. Wherever she goes, howls of laughter follow. Yesterday in Tolucca market, she wanted to fill out her collection of pottery animals. She went to a puesta and said I want a bull (*quiero un toro*). That means I want a stud, colloquially. The whole market roared. Most of her pottery animals have flowers painted on them. The rat, instead of being embarrassed, pointed to me and said, *Segura, tengo un toro pero el no tiene flores en el estomago* (sure I have a bull but he had no flowers on his stomach). Then the market just fell to pieces. You could hear the roars of laughter go down the street as each person was told the story. Half an hour later they were still laughing. And when Carol bargains, a crowd collects. Indians from the country stand with their mouths open. The thing goes from gentle to fury to sorrow to despair. And everyone loves it. The seller as much as any one. . . .

    I like what one market woman said to Carol. Carol said, "I would like to buy this but I am not rich." And the market woman—"You have shoes and a hat, of course you are rich.". . .

love to annie

John

Al Cooper

A Chicago broker offers a few friendly words of warning to his customers who never find time for vacations:

"Enjoy yourself—It's Later Than You Think"

Dear Friend:

In 1923, a group of the world's most successful financiers met at the Edgewater Beach Hotel. Present were:

President of the largest independent steel company.
President of the largest utility company.
President of the New York Stock Exchange.
Member of the President's Cabinet.
The greatest "Bear" in Wall Street.
The head of the world's largest monopoly.

Collectively, these tycoons controlled more wealth than there was in the United States Treasury; and for years, newspapers and magazines have been printing their success stories and urging the Youth of the Nation to follow their examples.

Now, twenty-five years later, let's see what happened to these men:

The President of the largest independent steel company—Charles Schwab—lived on borrowed money the last five years of his life, and died broke.
The President of the largest utility company—Samuel Insull—penniless in his latter years.
The President of the New York Stock Exchange—Richard Whitney—spent more than three years in Sing Sing.
The member of the President's Cabinet—Albert Fall—was pardoned from prison so he could die at home.

The greatest "Bear" in Wall Street—Jessie
Livermore—committed suicide.

The head of the world's greatest monopoly "The
Match King"—at one time controlled a fortune of
hundreds of millions and died bankrupt after the
crash of 1929.

All of these men had learned how to make money, but not
one of them learned how to live.

That reminds me, I am now in Miami Beach, Florida and
expect to return in June. I intend to do a lot of fishing and boat-
ing, and in my spare time, I will fill in with gin-rummy and just
loafing in the sun. If you get down my way . . . I will enjoy seeing you.

Sincerely,

Al *Cooper*

P.S.   No matter how hard you try, you won't leave this world
alive.

Albert S. Kaloa, Jr., and Keith Funston

Of the many droll proposals the New York Stock Exchange received for relocating, this Indian chief's invitation must have been the drollest:

March 11, 1966

Mr. Keith Funston, President
New York Stock Exchange
New York City, New York

Dear Sir:

... We ... noted with interest that you contemplate a change of location.

The governing body of the Moquawkie Indian Reservation have passed a resolution by the terms of which they will build an exchange facility at Tyonek, Alaska at no expense to you ...

We will give you, the Exchange, and its members a tax free status for a period of not less than 100 years. ...

We ... point out that the jet age of tomorrow will take less time to fly from New York City to Tyonek, Alaska than to drive through the heavy traffic of New York City to its residential suburbs. ...

We have a firm policy of investing only within the state of Alaska, but should our location be acceptable to you, it is possible that we might consider an exchange facility in a different area but certainly not New York City. The Manhattan incident is a painful memory, and we still have a few of the beads, and we are somewhat amused that the white people are now reduced to skinning one another instead of skinning the Indians.

May we hear from you.

Yours truly,

Albert S. Kaloa, Jr.
Chief

Keith Funston, then president of the New York Stock Exchange, replied:

NEW YORK STOCK EXCHANGE
Eleven Wall Street
New York 5, N.Y.

March 25, 1966

Dear Mr. Kaloa:

May I express the Exchange's thanks to you for your most hospitable invitation to consider relocating our facilities in Tyonek. . . .

The grandeur of Alaska, and the kindness of your offer certainly need no endorsement from me. But, as one chief to another, I am a little concerned by your statement that you still have some of those seventeenth-century beads. This suggests a degree of financial acumen which makes me wonder who actually got skinned in the Manhattan real estate deal of 1626. . . .

Cordially,

G. *Keith Funston*
President

Stanley Marcus

After being treated most courteously at the famed Neiman-Marcus department store, an appreciative customer addressed this letter to Mr. Marcus:

Mr. Stanley Marcus
Neiman-Marcus
Dallas, Texas

Dear Mr. Marcus:

I have been receiving beautiful and expensive brochures from you at regular intervals. It occurs to me that you might divert a little of your fortune you must be spending for this advertising matter to raise the salaries of your more faithful employees. For instance, there's an unassuming, plainly dressed little man on the second floor who always treats me with extreme courtesy when I visit your store, and generally persuades me to buy something I don't really want. Why don't you pay him a little more? He looks as though he could use it.

Yours truly,

Mrs. W. S.

Mr. Marcus replied:

Dear Mrs. S.:

Your letter impressed us so deeply that we called a directors' meeting immediately, and thanks solely to your own solicitude, voted my father a twenty-dollar-a-week raise.

Yours truly,

Stanley Marcus

Los Alamos Laboratories

The Los Alamos scientific laboratories have a highly automated accounting department. One of the operators of the computer complex—with a rare sense of humor for an engineer—posted this warning:

Achtung! Alles Lookenspeepers:

Das computenmachine is nicht fur gefingerpoken und mittengraben. Ist easy schnappen der springenwerk, blowenfusen, und poppencorken mit pittzensparken. Ist nicht fur gewerken by das dummkopfen. Das rubbernecken sightseeren keepen hans in das pockets—relaxen und vatch das blinkenlights.

Los Alamos National Laboratories

Necci Sales Manager

A despairing wife sent this letter to "Dear Abby":

Dear Abby:

For my forty-fifth wedding anniversary my husband bought me a plot in the cemetery. Now maybe I shouldn't have said all the things I did to him, but how would you have felt if you were expecting a sewing machine?

A sympathizing sewing machine sales manager replied:

Dear Abby:

With regard to that woman whose husband bought her a plot in the cemetery when she wanted a sewing machine. Tell her we'll make a deal with her. We'll give her a sewing machine free if she'll give us the plot. I think some of our salesmen are dead!

Necci Sewing Machine Sales Manager

Buttery Words

Competition is keen for advertising copywriters' jobs, but this letter won for its writer an immediate place on the payroll of a leading New York agency:

Gentlemen:

I like fat, buttery words; such as ooze, turpitude, glutinous, toady. I like solemn, angular, creaky words; such as straitlaced, cantankerous, pecunious, valedictory. I like spurious, gold-plated, black-is-white words; such as gentlefolk, mortician, free-lancer, mistress. I like suave "V" words; such as Svengali, svelte, bravura, verve. I like crunchy, brittle, crackly words; such as splinter, grapple, justle, crusty. I like sullen, crabbed, scowling words; such as skulk, glower, scabby, churl. I like oh-heavens, my-gracious, land's-sake words; such as tricksy, tucker, genteel, horrid. I like pretty, flowered, endimanché words; such as elegant, halcyon, Elysium, artiste. I like wormy, squirmy, mealy words; such as crawl, blubber, squeal, drip. I like sniggly, chuckling words; such as cowlick, gurgle, bubble, and burp.

I like words. May I have a few with you?

Name Withheld

William Safire

Word expert William Safire, in his book *On Language*, writes, "Whenever I get a note headed 'From the desk of . . . ,' I am inclined to sizzle back something like this":

Dear Mr. So and So:

Tell your desk, which has written to me recently in your name, that it should clean itself out and stop trying to pass itself off as a source of correspondence.

William Safire

John D. Yeck

John D. Yeck, cleverest of writers of sales letters, also conducts the monthly mailings of the "Let's Have Better Mottoes Association." Among our favorites are these timely mottoes for the new year:

Dear Mr. Lang:

In enthusiastic preparation for end of year celebrations and as part of the national effort to discourage too much of same, the Directors have chosen a motto that is perilously close to being "inspirational" and, therefore, ineligible, but nevertheless barely slipped by . . .

People who live in stone houses }
shouldn't throw glasses.

WORD PLAY

And—man's best friend is the hot dog. It feeds the hand that bites it.

And—middle age is when you hear "snap, pop, crackle" without eating cereal.

Other mottoes faintly fitting the season include: "Youth is when you're allowed to stay up 'til midnight new year's eve: middle age is when you're forced to" . .

To get a job well done, give it to a busy man. His secretary will do it.

Cordially,

John D. Yeck
Secretary

Hotel Manager

When a vacationer wrote to a hotel asking whether they permitted dogs in their rooms, the manager sent this welcomed reply:

Dear Sir,

I've been in the hotel business over 30 years. Never yet have I called the police to eject a disorderly dog during the small hours of the night. Never yet has a dog set the bed-clothes afire from smoking a cigarette. I've never found a hotel towel or blanket in a dog's suitcase, nor whisky rings on the bureau top from a dog's bottle. Sure the dog's welcome.

The Manager

P.S.   If he'll vouch for you, come along, too.

Anson H. Beard and Steve Collins

After Kohlberg, Kravis & Roberts' record-breaking takeover of Nabisco RJR, *Time* magazine reported that Henry Kravis stated reassuringly, "Oreos will still be in our children's lunch boxes." Two skeptical *Time* readers sent this note to the editor:

Concord, Massachusetts

Dear Sir:

Oreos may continue to be in children's lunch boxes, but they will already show bite marks.

Anson H. Beard
Steve Collins

Maron Simon

If you ever have engaged in a spirited battle for a restaurant check—and who hasn't?—you will appreciate this note once received by Bernard H. Schulist, former president of the Continental Bank, from a New York friend:

Dear Bernie:

We look forward to having dinner with you on Friday, October 26. We can have it at home, in a restaurant, or even pack a lunch and eat it in an airport-terminal phone booth. This being my "hometown" for well nigh on to thirty years, I expect you to be my guest, which naturally you will be if we have dinner at home; this without argument. If we go out to dinner the same direction of hospitality prevails; you to be my guest. This of course is going to provoke the same packet of protests that have ensued practically every time I've seen you here, so I will tell you herewith that I have reached the stage at which I am no longer willing to court cardiac catastrophe for the sake of protocol. I will pay, or you can pay, or we can match for it, or have separate checks, or cast lots, draw straws, or Indian-wrestle. What the hell difference does it make, so long as we're together.

See you next week.

Maron

19 October 1956

XVIII

Clerical Wit

Sydney Smith
Duke of Wellington
Joseph Chamberlain
Dr. S. Parker Cadman
Vatican Secretary
Kentucky Parson
Richard C. Lee
Bliss Perry
Henry Ward Beecher
Unnamed Minister
Thomas H. Huxley
Myles W. Edwards

DEF

Letter writing is the only device for combining solitude and good company.
—*Lord Byron*

DEAR WIT

Sydney Smith

Even invitations from the witty English clergyman Sydney Smith were never dull and routine. This is how he invited the Irish poet Thomas Moore to join him for breakfast and conversation:

Dear Moore,

I have a breakfast of philosophers tomorrow at ten punctually; muffins and metaphysics, crumpets and contradiction. Will you come?

Sydney Smith

Duke of Wellington

The Duke of Wellington, hero of the Battle of Waterloo, once received this letter from his brother-in-law, Henry Pakenham, Dean of Armagh:

My Dear Arthur,

A word from you will make me a Bishop.

Yours affectionately,

Henry

The "Iron" Duke replied:

Not a word.

Yours affectionately,

Wellington

Joseph Chamberlain

When Joseph Chamberlain was Colonial Secretary, he received a communique from the Island of Malta, saying certain monks were violating their vows. By a slip of the keys, the message came through; the monks have been violating their cows. Chamberlain noted:

PUN Clearly this is a case for a Papal Bull.

Colonial Secretary

Dr. S. Parker Cadman

The well-known clergyman, S. Parker Cadman, once received this query from a religious youth:

Dear Doctor Cadman,

Is it possible to lead a good Christian life in New York City on eighteen dollars a week?

Unnamed Youth

The kindly and quick-witted clergyman replied:

My dear boy,

That's about all you can do.

Dr. Cadman

Vatican Secretary

The briefest of all letters is that of the Vatican secretary, responding to a foreign missionary, who had requested permission to return to Ireland to see his dying mother. The secretary granted the request with the imperative mood of the Latin word meaning, "Go Thou":

Father Patrick

i

Papal Secretary of the State

Kentucky Parson

Failing to get action on an unpaid bill owed by a small-town Kentucky tradesman, a Paducah wholesaler sent letters to the railroad station agent of the town, asking if the goods had been delivered. He also wrote to the president of the local bank inquiring about the man's credit, and to the mayor asking the name of a good lawyer, in case he had to bring suit. As Alben Barkley tells the story in "That Reminds Me," the debtor himself replied as follows:

Dear Sir:

As station agent of this town, I am glad to advise you that the goods were delivered. As president of the local bank, it gives me pleasure to inform you that my credit is good. As mayor of the town, I am compelled to advise you that I am the only lawyer here. And if it were not for the fact that I am also pastor of the Baptist church, I would tell you to go to h---!

I. M. D.

Richard C. Lee

After giving a talk on urban renewal, Richard C. Lee, the mayor of New Haven, Connecticut, received this letter from an irate citizen:

Mayor Lee,

You couldn't be further off base. When you run again, I wouldn't vote for you if you were Saint Peter.

Mrs. ———

The mayor retorted:

Dear Madam,

If I were Saint Peter, you wouldn't be in my voting district.

Richard C. Lee, Mayor

Bliss Perry

Bliss Perry, who taught English to two generations of Harvard students, was a gentle soul who was reluctant to say an unkind word about anyone. Asked for a recommendation for a clergyman who was told to leave when his congregation could not get him to resign, Perry wrote:

My dear Mr. Williamson:

Rev. Mr. ———, about whom you inquire, is a gentleman and a scholar. He has all the Christian virtues except resignation.

Bliss Perry

Henry Ward Beecher

The Reverend Henry Ward Beecher was the brother of Harriet Beecher Stowe who wrote *Uncle Tom's Cabin*. After delivering one of his popular sermons, the Reverend received this poison-pen letter:

Dear Beecher:

I journeyed from my New York hotel yesterday morning to hear you preach, expecting, of course, to hear an exposition of the gospel of Jesus Christ. Instead, I heard a political harangue with no reason or cohesion in it. You made an ass of yourself.

Name withheld

The Reverend Beecher replied:

Dear Sir,

. . . I am sorry, . . . that you think I made an ass of myself. In this connection I have but one consolation: that you didn't make an ass of *yourself*. The Lord did that.

Henry Ward Beecher

Unnamed Minister

One Sunday, a minister appearing before his congregation with a bandage on his face, explained: "I was thinking about my sermon while shaving and cut my face." After delivering an unusually long sermon, the clergyman found this unsigned note in the collection plate.

Next time, why not think about your face and cut the sermon.

Thomas Huxley

When the absent-minded Matthew Arnold walked off with author-biologist Thomas Huxley's umbrella, Arnold received this witty reminder:

My dear Arnold:

Look at Bishop Wilson on the sin of covetousness and then inspect your umbrella stand. You will there see a beautiful brown smooth-handled umbrella which is not your property. Think of what the excellent prelate would have advised and bring it with you next time you come to the club.

Ever yours faithfully,

T. H. *Huxley*

Myles W. Edwards

This letter from a rector to his bishop appeared in the bulletin of the Episcopal Church of the Good Shepherd in Hemet, California:

The Rt. Rev. William H. Mead:

Some time ago I wrote to inform you that one of our young boys who was confirmed in January took his confirmation gift money and bought a collared lizard, which he named Bishop in your honor. A little later he bought a smaller lizard, and named it Rector in my honor. I thought you would be interested to know that I recently received a report that the Bishop ate the Rector.

Sincerely,

Myles W. Edwards
Rector

XIX

Doctors' and Patients' Wit

Dr. Alexander Guemot

Dr. J. M. Mackintosh

Dr. Anton Chekhov

Doctor X

Dr. Oliver Wendell Holmes

George Reedy

Dr. Shelbe

Dr. Allen S. Johnson

Honorary Physician

Abigail Van Buren

Dr. Stephen Kaufman

Bob Hope

Hilarie Brown

George Burns

These ink stains ... possess a strange charm to penetrate and stir the deepest feelings of those privileged to read them.
—*Charles Reade*

Dr. Alexander Guemot

Dr. Alexander Guemot writes mournfully to a friend announcing the birth of a son. The doctor's pessimistic words, written more than a century and a half ago, remind us that we have no monopoly on bemoaning the times:

April, 1832

Dear Friend Guy:

I do not know whether to be happy or sorry over the birth of a son to which I have contributed only a modest share. The poor infant enters the world in a very troubled time.

Hardly 17 years have passed since peace was restored to Europe, and we still suffer cruelly from the effects of the war. Who knows if my son will not one day be forced to become the citizen of a republic? It makes one shudder. The conditions of life are daily becoming more difficult. Nanette, our servant, has paid 23 sous (7 3/4c) for half a kilo of butter and 2 sous (2/3c) for each fresh egg. It is absurd and exorbitant.

I would like to see my son embracing the noble career of medicine, but I see quite well that he cannot. One of the heads of the faculty has confided to me that this profession is literally invaded, and then this madness of speed is wearing out men. Only yesterday I saw a post chaise tearing along. It makes one giddy. The horses were galloping at more than five leagues an hour and everyone wants his carriage.

The streets of Paris are so congested that you must wait a long time if you wish to cross them. Madness of the century, my dear friend, for which men will pay in the brevity of their days! My son, like his contemporaries, will not live to be old. We know not what the future has in store for him, but we can bet with certainty on his not becoming a centenarian.

Yours,

Guemot

Editor's Note: Not only did the son about whom this letter was written live to be a centenarian, but he was honored on his one-hundredth birthday by The French Academy of Medicine.

Dr. J. M. Mackintosh

Dr. J. M. Mackintosh, eminent British physician, charmingly addressed this letter to himself in 1933, with instructions to open it twenty-three years later, on his sixty-fifth birthday.

6th March, 1933

My dear Mackintosh,

I hesitate to call you by your Christian name, because I do not know you well enough. All the same, I think you may profit by a few words of friendly advice. Certain undesirable tendencies in your character and outlook are already apparent; and I have little doubt that they will become more marked as you grow older.

In the first place, you will become more talkative. . . . Try to be a good listener as you grow older; it is well worth your pains. . . .

Secondly, do not get suspicious of people and their motives; and avoid especially prying into the affairs of young folk . . . If they ask for help in time of trial, give it in full measure, but don't imagine that the so-called wisdom acquired by you from experience will help *them*, unless they feel the need.

Thirdly, do not try to attract sympathy to yourself. Do not pose as the dear old man, in the hope of hearing affectionate murmurs that you are young in spirit. For God's sake be a real person, with a valuation that does not need artificial boosting. There are three qualities that you can develop as you grow older: they are courtesy, tolerance, and integrity, which together make an understanding spirit. . . .

The main practical thing to remember, however, is that you are now sixty-five and on the point of retirement. For heaven's sake retire and do not persuade yourself that you are a special case. If you have kept mind and body active, a world of new interests lies before you. . . .

As we grow older, self-criticism tends to become blunted. I know of no better test than the one proposed by George Meredith:

"You may estimate your capacity for comic perception by being able to detect the ridicule of them you love, without loving them less; and more by being able to see yourself somewhat ridiculous in dear eyes, and accepting the correction their image of you proposes."

Now remember . . .

Yours faithfully,

James M. Mackintosh

After reading this twenty-three-year-old letter on his sixty-fifth birthday, Dr. Mackintosh penned the following reply to his younger self:

20th February, 1956

My dear Mackintosh,

Many thanks for your letter of twenty-three years ago. I opened it as you directed, on my sixty-fifth birthday. A little solemn, I thought—but then, of course, you were addressing a man old enough to be your father.

The plain truth is that I must not make a virtue of necessity: I retire at sixty-five, and that's that. I am not a special case. Thanks all the same for your friendly advice which I shall try humbly to follow. It has been such fun since you wrote . . .

Yours truly,

J. M. Mackintosh

Dr. Anton Chekhov

Anton Chekhov was a physician as well as a dramatist and short story writer. As his plays and stories became more popular, his editor-publisher asked why he did not concentrate on his literary efforts. Chekhov wittily explained:

To A. S.
Moscow. September 11, 1888.

Dear Souvorin,

. . . You advise me not to hunt after two hares, and not to think of medical work. I do not know why one should not hunt two hares even in the literal sense. . . I feel more confident and more satisfied with myself when I reflect that I have two professions and not one. Medicine is my lawful wife and literature is my mistress. When I get tired of one I spend the night with the other. Though it's disorderly, it's not so dull, and besides, neither of them loses anything from my infidelity. If I did not have my medical work, I doubt if I could have given my leisure and my spare thoughts to literature. There is no discipline in me.

Chekhov

Doctor X

When an alarmed optician closed his office and escaped from Nazi Germany to the West, he left this notice for his patients:

To My Patients:

The nearsighted should go to the eye clinic.
The farsighted should follow me.

Doctor X

Dr. Oliver Wendell Holmes

When Confederate emissaries Mason and Slidell were seized aboard a British vessel during the Civil War, the *Boston Herald* published a letter from a Southern sympathizer expressing the fear that the act would "sever the umbilical cord that bound America to the Mother Country." Dr. Oliver Wendell Holmes, then professor of anatomy at Harvard, wrote to the editor as follows:

Dear Sir:

The gentleman who wrote to you, expressing the fear that the Mason and Slidell affair might result in the severance of the umbilical cord that has heretofore bound America to the mother country, is quite right. But I would go even farther and say that such result might mean the end of England's *navel* supremacy.

Oliver Wendell Holmes

George Reedy

Beefy George Reedy, one-time White House press secretary, was ordered by his doctor to the hospital to lose weight. When some White House aids sent him flowers, Reedy sent them this thank you note:

Thank you for the flowers.
They were delicious.

Reedy

Dr. Shelbe

When the wife of a patient was disturbed by personality changes in her husband, she sent this letter to his doctor:

Dear Doctor,

My husband used to be a contented, happy family man, an ideal mate and father. Since consulting you, he has become restless, flirtatious, critical of my housekeeping and our children, an ogre about bills, vain, arrogant, and, I suspect, a woman-chaser. It is my belief that you have been giving him hormone shots which have entirely changed his personality . . .

Mrs. A. Jones

The doctor replied:

Dear Mrs. Jones,

In response to your letter, I have not been giving your husband shots of any kind. I have had him fitted with contact lenses.

Dr. Shelbe

Dr. Allen S. Johnson

After a London physician diagnosed Mona Lisa's inscrutable smile as being due to her pregnant condition, an American doctor offered a different theory:

Editor
New England Journal
of Medicine

Dear Sir:

To one unencumbered by the sophistication of the obstetricians and historians, that smug, sly smile can have only one explanation: Mona Lisa has just discovered that she is *not* pregnant.

Dr. Allen S. Johnson

Honorary Physician

When a doctor was appointed Honorary Physician to the Queen of England, he received this telegram from a joshing associate:

CONGRATULATIONS.
GOD SAVE THE QUEEN!

Abigail Van Buren

As tax time approached, a cautious and frugal-minded reader sent this query to advice-columnist Abigail Van Buren. From the book, *The Best of Dear Abby*:

Dear Abby:

Are birth control pills deductible?

Kay

Never at a loss for clever repartee, Abby replied:

Dear Kay:

Only if they don't work.

Abby

Dr. Stephen Kaufman

The late Carl J. Koch was the doting owner of a poodle named Gidget. From abroad came a post card, picturing two poodles, addressed to Gidget with this message in the minute handwriting of grandson Dr. Stephen Kaufman:

Dear Gidget,

Being near France, I decided to search for your long lost relatives, and I found two and heard of others. Your mother, *Digit*, I am sad to say, was killed in a terrible fight with a Yorkshire Terrier in a dispute involving a ball's ownership. Your father, *Gadget*, has not been seen since he ran off into the hills, terrified by his shadow on a sunny day. Your elder brother, *Widget*, was badly hurt when he ran into a tree trying to escape a menacing-looking kitten. He survived and fathered many pups, some of which have made tolerable pets. *Fidget*, (the black poodle) pictured on the right, is now regarded as the black sheep of the family, much to the relief of other members who feared that they would earn this title. He barks at everything that is immobile and of no apparent threat. He made fast friends wth a burglar who broke in while his master was out. The great news is I have found your long lost twin sister, *Midget*, pictured on the left. She snarls at everyone and everything, but never bites. If meticulously groomed, she does not look quite as shabby as in this picture. Like many in her family, she suffers from halitosis. Also typical, she is very loyal, very intelligent, and she has complete comprehension of the native tongue, but she has difficulty speaking it. All were distressed to hear that you were spayed—a loss for all dogkind. They were pleased to hear about your nice master and they were envious. All send their fondest regards.

Steve

Bob Hope

In his book *Have Tux, Will Travel*, Bob Hope recalls the time he was thrown seven feet from a prop horse, while making the film *Fancy Pants*. Hope was rushed to the hospital with a badly injured back. Some weeks later, he wrote to Henry Ginsberg, then head of Paramount Studios:

Dear Henry:

I want to thank you for your kindness during my recent illness and tell you that you did not have to do it, I wasn't going to sue . . . Inasmuch as you are going to have to explain my $4,500 doctor bills at the next stockholders' meeting (assuming you are still with the company), I think I should explain that they are not out of line.

You and I know that in the old days when a man fell on his back, he got up, tightened his belt, and walked back into the bar . . . But medicine has made great strides during our generation. When I woke up in the hospital, four nurses were standing over me, a doctor was feeling my pulse, and a specialist was busy on the phone checking with the bank to see how much we would go for.

Then they started the tests which you find on Page Three of the bill . . . Meantime, no one would tell me how I was doing. Finally I picked up the phone, got an outside wire, called the hospital, and asked how Bob Hope was doing. I'd taken a turn for the worse . . . We've sure come a long ways from sulphur and molasses.

Bob

Hilarie Brown

A doctor received payment for his bill, with some polite but pointed questions about treatments rendered to the female patient:

March 4, 1960

Dear Doctor Harper:

I enclose my check in payment for last month's statement, but have a few questions about it. We understood that house calls are only $5 each—did the two house calls on February 8th and 10th include Trudi's penicillin shots? And what about that item, "Treat ent."? I can't remember having called "ent." Mr. Brown says perhaps this is the medical term for eczema, but didn't we bring her in for that back in December?

We are delighted with Trudi's progress since the tonsillectomy, and feel that the fee is very fair, indeed. Is the extra charge for the anesthetist or for the oral surgeon who extracted those baby teeth during the operation? It really doesn't matter; we're just curious.

Thank you for any explanation you can give us. We'll be seeing you in a few weeks when Trudi has her puppies.

Very truly yours,

Hilarie Brown

George Burns

George Burns receives hundreds of letters asking for his advice. His answers are among the funniest:

Dear George,

I am a senior citizen, and they tell me I should be enjoying the Golden Years. How can I awake every morning with a song in my heart?

Still Kicking

Burns replied:

Dear Still,

Try an AM-FM pacemaker.

George

———

X X

Legal Wit

———
———

Madame de Sévigné
Robert Louis Stevenson
Abraham Lincoln
Judge Robert L. Bensing
Judge Isaacs
Felix Frankfurter
Elbert Hamlin

Letters, such as are written by wise men, are, of all the words of men, in my judgment the best.
—*Francis Bacon*

DEAR WIT

Madame de Sévigné

Reputed to be one of the greatest letter writers, Madame de Sévigné threatens to sue Judge Phillipe Moulceau for neglecting their friendship. She tells of the marriage of her grandson to a wealthy but socially inferior heiress. Explaining the misalliance, the bride's mother-in-law was heard to say, "Even the best lands need manuring":

June 5, 1695

Dear Monsieur,

I intend, Monsieur, to bring suit against you. Here is how I shall proceed. I intend to have you judge it yourself. It is more than a year since I came here to be with my daughter for whom I still feel a strong affinity. You must, doubtlessly, since then, have heard talk about the marriage of the Marquis de Grignan to Mademoiselle de Saint-Amans. You have seen her often enough at Montpellier to know what she is like. You will also have heard talk about her father's great wealth. . . .

Have you forgotten us? Is it indifference on your part? I know that you are in good health. What do you expect me to think? What is the meaning of your conduct? Give it a name, Monsieur. And that is the suit I bring against you. It is for you to judge. I consent, as you can see, to your being both judge and defendant.

Marquise de Sévigné

Editor's Note: The original, full text of this letter is in the Frances and H. Jack Lang Collection at Case Western Reserve University.

Robert Louis Stevenson

Robert Louis Stevenson agreed to trade his birthday for the birthday of little Annie Ide. Born on Christmas Day, Annie was "defrauded of her natural rights to a private anniversary of her own," observed RLS:

Vailima, June 19, 1891

I, Robert Louis Stevenson, Advocate of the Scots Bar, author of *The Master of Ballantrae* and *Moral Emblems*, stuck civil engineer, sole owner and patentee of the Palace and Plantation known as Vailima in the island of Upolu, Samoa, a British subject, being in sound mind, and pretty well, I thank you, in body:

In consideration that Miss Annie H. Ide, daughter of H. C. Ide, the town of Saint Johnsbury, in the county of Caledonia, in the state of Vermont, United States of America, was born, out of all reason, upon Christmas Day, and is therefore out of all justice denied the consolation and profit of a proper birthday; . . .

And considering that I, the said Robert Louis Stevenson, have attained an age when, O, we never mention it, and that I have now no further use for a birthday of any description . . .

Have *transferred*, and do *hereby transfer*, to the said Annie H. Ide, *all and whole* my rights and privileges in the thirteenth day of November, formerly my birthday, now, hereby and henceforth, the birthday of the said Annie H. Ide, to have, hold, exercise, and enjoy the same in the customary manner, by the sporting of fine raiment, eating of rich meats, and receipt of gifts, compliments, and copies of verse, according to the manner of our ancestors . . .

In witness whereof I have hereto set my hand and seal this nineteenth day of June in the year of grace eighteen hundred and ninety-one.

Robert Louis Stevenson

Abraham Lincoln

When a young attorney, opposing Abraham Lincoln, lacked sufficient funds to stay in Springfield until a case came up, Lincoln agreed to argue both sides. After the trial, Honest Abe wrote his young adversary announcing the Judge's decision:

My dear Mr. Bishop:

The Supreme Court came in on the appointed day and I did my best to keep faith with you. Apparently I argued your case better than my own, for the court has just sent down a rescript in your favor. Accept my heartiest congratulations.

Very sincerely yours,

A. *Lincoln*

Judge Robert L. Bensing

On the office wall of Judge Robert L. Bensing in the Hobbs, New Mexico City Hall, appears this waspish note addressed to all visitors:

While in this office, speak in a low, soothing tone and do not disagree with me in any manner.

Please be informed that when one has reached my age, noise and nonconcurrence cause gastric hyperperistalsis, hypersecretion of hydrochloric acid and inflammation of the gastric mucosa, and

I BECOME UNPLEASANT.

Judge Robert L. Bensing

Judge Isaacs

Before an accused was about to be tried in his court, New York Judge Isaacs received this letter:

Dear Judge,

The clerk of your court told me I could have a lawyer represent me but I do not need one, the Lord is my advocate.

Unnamed Defendant

Judge Isaacs replied:

Dear Sir,

I still feel you should have someone locally.

Judge Isaacs

Felix Frankfurter

Supreme Court Justice Felix Frankfurter explained to the chairman of a banquet committee, the conditions of his acceptance of an invitation to serve as toastmaster:

Dear Sir:

Please remember that I am to be merely, as it were, the showman—the "Balieff of the Chauve Souris." In addition, my task will be that of timekeeper, and I shall be admonished to convey with sweet persuasiveness that, at least for the duration of the banquet, time is finite and not infinite. I shall be admonished also to remind the speakers of a rather canny injunction in the Talmud, when it suggests that at funerals the orators should bear in mind that there is a judgment day, not alone for the deceased, but also for the orators.

Felix Frankfurter

Elbert Hamlin

Teaching astronomy at Yale, William Beebe flunked Elbert Hamlin for giving too many moons to Saturn. Fifteen years later, Hamlin, then a distinguished judge, learned of the discovery of several additional moons and wrote to Professor Beebe:

Professor William Beebe
Yale University
New Haven, Connecticut

Dear Professor,

Fifteen years ago you flunked me not knowing that my knowledge of Saturn exceeded yours. And your flunking me was a tragedy for Yale. There was the golden opportunity which would have given Yale University immortality in science by announcing a discovery fifteen years ahead of all other institutions of learning. I can forgive you for the personal insult, but it is difficult to forgive you when we remember what my discovery would have meant in adding prestige to Yale.

Elbert Hamlin

XXI

Wit That Is Wisdom

Lord Chesterfield
Robert G. Ingersoll
Albert Einstein
H. L. Mencken
Edward Everett
George Jessel
Brendan Behan
Armenian Radio Station
Jean Cocteau
"Kup" Kupcinet
E. B. White
Miss Manners
Philip A. Davies

The chief interest of a study of the great letter writers is that it introduces us not to literary works, but to persons.

—*Sir Walter Raleigh*

Lord Chesterfield

Lord Chesterfield is best known for his letters of scholarly advice to his natural son—advice given in vain because the son never lived up to the position for which his father was preparing him. This is one of Lord Chesterfield's more light-hearted anecdotes:

London, December 11, O.S. 1747

Dear Boy,

There is nothing which I more wish that you should know, and which fewer people do know, than the true use and value of Time. . . .

I knew a gentleman, who was so good a manager of his time, that he would not even lose that small portion of it which the calls of nature obliged him to pass along in the necessary-house, but gradually went through all the Latin poets in those moments. He bought, for example, a common edition of Horace, of which he tore off gradually a couple of pages, carried them with him to that necessary place, read them first, and then sent them down as a sacrifice to Cloacina: This was so much time fairly gained; and I recommend to you to follow his example. It is better than only doing what you cannot help doing at those moments; and it will make any book which you shall read in that manner, very present to your mind . . .

Chesterfield

Robert G. Ingersoll

Robert G. Ingersoll, son of a minister, was known as "the greatest agnostic." An eloquent orator and writer, Ingersoll sings the praises of a present he is giving to his son-in-law to be:

89 Fifth Avenue
New York, April 16, 1887

Walston H. Brown Esq.

My dear Friend,

I send you some of the most wonderful whiskey that ever drove the skeleton from a feast or painted landscapes in the brain of man. It is the mingled souls of wheat and corn. There are in it the sunshine and shadows that chased each other over the billowy fields—the breath of June—the carol of the lark—the dews of night—the wealth of summer and autumn's rich content—all golden with imprisoned light.

Drink it—and you will hear the voices of men and maidens singing the Harvest Home, mingled with the laughter of children.

Drink it—and you will feel within your blood the star-lit dawns, the dreamy, tawny dusks of many perfect days.

For forty years this liquid joy has been within the happy staves of oak, longing to touch the lips of men.

Yours always,

R. G. Ingersoll

Albert Einstein

When a conservative Women's League protested against Albert Einstein's first visit to America, calling him a Socialist, Einstein wittily addressed the disapproving ladies with this letter:

To The American Women's League,

Never yet have I experienced from the fair sex such energetic rejection of all advances; or, if I have, never from so many at once.

But are they not quite right, these watchful citizenesses? Why should one open one's doors to a person who devours hard-boiled capitalists with as much appetite and gusto as the Cretan Minotaur in days gone by devoured luscious Greek maidens, and on top of that is low-down enough to reject every sort of war, except the unavoidable war with one's own wife? Therefore give heed to your clever and patriotic womenfolk and remember that the Capitol of mighty Rome was once saved by the cackling of its faithful geese.

Albert Einstein

H. L. Mencken

In his will, the ever witty H. L. Mencken included this formula for pleasing his ghost:

If after I depart this vale, you ever remember to please my ghost, forgive some sinner and wink your eye at a homely girl.

H. L. *Mencken*

Edward Everett

Edward Everett was the Harvard president who delivered the principle oration at Gettysburg. Abraham Lincoln gave a brief address. Asked for his advice by an indignant Bostonian about suing a newspaper that had libelled him, Everett replied:

Dear Sir:

What should you do? My dear sir, do nothing. Half the people who read that paper never saw that article. Half of those who did see it, failed to read it. Half of those who read it did not understand it. Half of those who understood it did not believe it. Half of those who believed it were of no consequence anyway.

Edward Everett

George Jessel

Actor and humorist George Jessel tells the editor of *Time* why he wisely opposes public hearings on TV:

Los Angeles
December 18, 1964

Dear Sir,

In regard to whether or not public hearings should be televised, I offer my authoritative opinion: there should be no such intimacy going on. In campaigns America has already been drugged into measuring only what the candidate looks and sounds like, not the importance of what he puts on paper. It frightens me to think what would have happened if TV had been as influential in the time of Socrates, who was not very pretty; or of Moses, who had a great impediment of speech; or of Jesus, whose Hebrew had a strong Galilean accent; or of Lincoln, whose wart, beard, and shrill voice would have made Madison Avenue get rid of him immediately. It was what Mr. Lincoln said at Gettysburg that will be remembered, not how he looked or sounded on television.

George Jessel

Brendan Behan

Another astute letter to the editor of *Time* came from the pen of salty, Irish playwright Brendan Behan:

Dublin, 1959

Dear Sir:

I enjoyed reading about myself and my wife in *Time*, but the nicest thing of all happened when a foreign citizen turned around from looking at my picture and said, "I did not realize you were Jewish." "I am not," I said, "but Our Blessed Lord is— I hope I've caught a little of the contagion."

Brendan Behan

Armenian Radio Station

The most popular jokes in Moscow take the form of letters to the Armenian Radio Station near the Russian border. Carl Mydans, veteran *Life* photographer, brought this one back from a trip to the Russian capital:

Dear Armenian Radio Station:

Can you tell me the difference between capitalism and communism?

Comrade

Dear Comrade:

Under capitalism, man exploits man.
Under communism, it is just the reverse.

Armenian Radio Station

WORD
PLAY

Jean Cocteau

Noting that some reference books give the birth date of Jean Cocteau as 1891, while others say 1892, the editor of the *American College Dictionary* wrote to the French poet-dramatist for clarification. Cocteau replied as follows:

Dear Sir,

This is exact: I was born the 5th of July, 1889, at the Laffitte House. I have seen that the *Larousse Dictionary* restores me to my youth. Let us console ourselves. Picasso says: "One puts in a very long time in order to become young."

Yours,

Jean Cocteau

"Kup" Kupcinet

"Kup" Kupcinet, popular columnist of the *Chicago Tribune*, offered this paradoxical advice to one of his readers:

Confidential to Herb M. ———

I don't know who said it first, but to achieve the ultimate in happiness one should practice moderation in all things. Including moderation.

Kupcinet

E. B. White

The always articulate E. B. White winds the clock as a symbol of his optimism for the future state of the world:

North Brooklin, Maine
30 March 1973

Dear Mr. Nadeau:

As long as there is one upright man, as long as there is one compassionate woman, the contagion may spread and the scene is not desolate. Hope is the thing that is left to us, in a bad time. I shall get up Sunday morning and wind the clock, as a contribution to order and steadfastness.

Sailors have an expression about the weather: they say, the weather is a great bluffer. I guess the same is true of our human society—things can look dark, then a break shows in the clouds, and all is changed, sometimes rather suddenly. It is quite obvious that the human race has made a queer mess of life on this planet. But as a people we probably harbor seeds of goodness that have lain for a long time waiting to sprout when the conditions are right. Man's curiosity, his relentlessness, his inventiveness, his ingenuity have led him into deep trouble. We can only hope that these same traits will enable him to claw his way out.

Hang on to your hat. Hang on to your hope. And wind the clock, for tomorrow is another day.

Sincerely,

E. B. White

Miss Manners

Asked how one acquires an interesting personality, advice columnist Miss Manners (Judith Martin), replied with sage counsel:

Dear Madam,

A lady who had as dinner partners on successive evenings the two great Victorian prime ministers, Gladstone and Disraeli, was asked to compare them. After sitting next to Gladstone, she reported, "I came away persuaded that he was the most fascinating person on earth." After sitting next to Disraeli, "I came away persuaded that I was the most fascinating person on earth."

Guess which one Queen Victoria was crazy about.

Miss Manners

Philip A. Davies

The London *Times* ran a series of suggested complimentary closes on letters for special occasions. British writer Philip A. Davies nominated Evelyn Waugh's standard sign-off as the best.

13 August 1982

Sir,

I have always thought of Evelyn Waugh's immortal phrase, "with love or what you will," as the ultimate end to my correspondence.

It has disarmed my sternest critic and redeemed my dullest prose.

Yours faithfully,

Philip A. Davies

About the Editor

H. Jack Lang is the retired founder and president of one of Cleveland's largest advertising agencies. He has edited or authored the following six books: *The Wit and Wisdom of Abraham Lincoln*; *Letters of the Presidents*, Freedom Foundation Medal winnner; *Lincoln's Fireside Reading*, Freedom Foundation Medal winner; *Two Kinds of Christmases*; *The Rowfant Manuscripts*, named one of the best books of the year by the American Institute of Graphic Arts; and *Letters in American History*.

Lang also is a collector of autograph letters. (His important collection was given to the Freiberger Library of Case Western Reserve University.) He has edited *The Wolf Magazine of Letters* for more than fifty years.

Acknowledgments

The editor wishes to acknowledge, first and foremost, the valuable assistance of Lynn Kaperak-Miller, who spent countless hours preparing the original and all additions to the manuscript and in researching and editing the same. Appreciation is also due David Guralnik, Editor Emeritus of *Webster's New World Dictionary*, for his encouragement and help in obtaining consideration of the manuscript.

In addition to Lynn Kaperak-Miller, the following joined in extensive efforts to obtain permissions from copyright owners to reprint letters: Cherine Demerdache, Sallie Sofranko, Nina Gagliardo, Dorothy Kraushaar and Kathleen Mackin. Finding the copyright owners of letters selected in *The Wolf Magazine of Letters* over a fifty-five year period, turned out to be a formidable task. Many of the letters are in public domain; others qualify for "fair use." A sizeable number came from magazine and book publishers now extinct. Some were contributed to The Wolf Magazine without identifying the source. Estates holding copyrights of deceased writers could not be located.

Despite the most diligent endeavors to search out copyright owners, many could not be found, or did not respond to our requests. To these, we apologize and hope to make amends in any future editions.

Nov. 19, 1991

No PEDAGOGIC WIT?

I—Biting Wit
Robert Ingersoll, from *William Feather Magazine*, circa 1914.
Mark Twain, reprinted from Twain's *Autobiography*, Harper Brothers, 1924, with the approval of the Trustees of the Mark Twain Foundation.
Henry James, from *Many Laughs for Many Days*, by Irvin F. Cobb, George H. Doran & Co.
Will Rogers, from *The Will Rogers Scrapbook*, edited by Brian B. Sterling, Grossett & Dunlap.
George Bernard Shaw, permission granted by The Society of Authors on behalf of the Bernard Shaw Estate.
Michael Noble M.P., from the letter column of *Campbeltown, Scotland Courier*.
Bertrand Russell, from the *American Scholar*, permission granted by Associate Editor Sandra Costich.
Pablo Picasso, from the *Diary of an Art Dealer*, by Rene Gimpel, Farrar, Straus & Giroux Inc.
Adlai Stevenson, from *The Stevenson Wit*, by Bill Adler, Doubleday & Co.
Unitas - Rickles, from Earl Wilson's column, circa 1975.

II—Boomerang Wit
Barrie - Housman, from *Coronet Magazine*, circa 1943.
Sari Maritza, from *Sari Maritza*, as told by Maurice Chevalier.
Woolcott - Cerf, from *A. Woolcott, His Life, His World*, World Publishing Co.
Dorothy Thompson, from "The Postage Stamp," The Marford Co.
Shaw - Churchill, permission granted by The Society of Authors on behalf of the Bernard Shaw Estate.
Shaw - Skinner, from *The Theater Arts Magazine*, with permission of The Society of Authors on behalf of the Bernard Shaw Estate.
Feldman - Korda, from *Reader's Scope*, circa 1945.
Lee Rosten, from *The World Of Leo Rosten*, Harper & Row.

III—Critical Wit
Alphonse Daudet, from *The Little Book of Famous Insults*, by Betty Jo Ramsey, Peter Pauper Press.
James Whitcomb Riley, from *Letters of James Whitcomb Riley*, edited by William Lyon Phelps, The Bobbs-Merrill Co., permission granted by Judith Fernandez, MacMillan Publishing Co.
Somerset Maugham, from *Pageant* magazine, circa 1956.
William Lyon Phelps, from *Anguished English*, by Richard Lederer, permission granted by Charles Wyrick, Jr. of Wyrick & Co.

IV—Gentle Wit
T. B. Aldrich, from *The Ladies Home Journal*, Meredith Corp.
Mark Twain, from *An Irreverent and Thoroughly Incomplete Social History of Practically Everything*, by Frank Muir, Stein & Day, with the approval of the Trustees of the Mark Twain Foundation.
H. G. Wells, from *2500 Anecdotes for All Occasions*, by Edmund Fuller, Avenel Books division of MacMillan Publishing Co.
Gelett Burgess, from *The New York Times*, circa 1942.
Ruth Van Bergen, from *Dear Hollywood*, edited by Juliet Lowell, Dell Publishing Co.
Vic Gelb, letter to the Cleveland City Club, permission granted by Victor Gelb.
Herman (Fritz) Liebert, letter to H. Jack Lang, permission granted by Herman Liebert.
Miss Manners, from *Miss Manners' Guide to Excruciatingly Correct Behavior*, Warner Books, Inc.

V—Authors' Wit
Nathaniel Hawthorne, from Woodrow Wilson International Center for Scholarship.
George Bernard Shaw, permission granted by The Society of Authors on behalf of the Bernard Shaw Estate.
Eugene O'Neill, from *The Biography of Eugene O'Neill*.
John Steinbeck, from *Steinbeck, A Life in Letters*, by Elaine Steinbeck and Robert Wallsten, Viking Press.
Bernard DeVoto, from "The Easy Chair," *Harper's Magazine*, October 26, 1950.
Erle Stanley Gardner, from *The Real Perry Mason*, by Dorothy Hughes, William Morrow & Co., permission granted by Lawrence Hughes.
P.G. Wodehouse, from *The Heart of a Goof*, H. Jenkins.

VI—Editors' Wit
Horace Greeley, from *New Current Digest*, circa 1936.
George Horace Lorimer, from *The Saturday Evening Post*.
William Allen White, from *The Emporia Gazette*, permission granted by Barbara White Walker of *The Emporia Gazette*.
H.L. Mencken, from Earl Wilson's column in *The Baltimore Sun*, permission granted by *The Baltimore Sun*.
Richard Watson Gilder, from *The Book of Modern Letters*, by Taintor & Monroe, MacMillan, Publishing Co.
Francis P. Church, from *The New York Sun*.
Bernard Kilgore, from *The Wall Street Journal*.

Harold Ross, permission granted by *The New Yorker*.
Newspaper Editor, from *Effective English*, by Edward Frank Allen, Fawcett Books Group.
Mason Walsh, from the *Associated Press Log*.

VII—Publishers' Wit
Jack London, from *Thessaurus of Anecdotes*, by Edmond Fuller, Avenel Books.
Edna St. Vincent Millay, letter to Cass Canfield of Harper & Row.
Groucho Marx, from *Variety Magazine*, reprinted by permission of Variety Inc. "Variety" is a registered trademark of Variety Inc.
Paul Brooks, imaginary letter of a publisher's editor from *The Atlantic Monthly*, permission granted by the author, Paul Brooks.

VIII—Autographic Wit
Rudyard Kipling, from *The Maranto Memo*, F & W Publications.
Marie Curie, from *The Little Book of Famous Insults*, by Betty Jo Ramsey, Peter Pauper Press, permission granted by Nick Beil, President of Peter Pauper Press.
Mark Twain, from *The Americanization of Edward Bok*, Charles Scribner & Sons, with the approval of the Trustees of the Mark Twain Foundation.
John F. Kennedy, from *Good Housekeeping*, circa 1963.
Peter DeVries, from *The Meaning of Life*, by Hugh Moorehead, The Chicago Review Press.

IX—Rhetorical Wit
Unnamed Author, from *Effective English*, by Edward Frank Allen, Fawcett Books Group.
Raymond Chandler, letter to editor Edward Weeks of *The Atlantic Monthly*, permission granted by Nancy Finn of *The Atlantic Monthly*.
Julian Huxley, letter dated August 17, 1938, from *Your Obedient Servant*, Rutledge, Chapman & Hall.
B. M. Starks, from *Time*.
Lester Aurbach, letter to H. Jack Lang, dated May 10, 1954, permission granted by Mrs. Lester P. Aurbach.
Marian Forer, letter dated July 30, 1964, from "Trade Winds" column of *The Saturday Review*.

X—Poetic Wit
John Donne, from *Undying Passion*, edited by Joseph Orgel, William Morrow.
Yuan Mel, from *The Golden Book Magazine*.
Lewis Carroll, from *A Second Treasury of the World's Great Letters*, by Brockway & Winer, permission granted by Simon & Schuster.
James Whitcomb Riley, letter dated 1892, from *The Letters of James Whitcomb Riley*, Bobbs-Merrill, permission granted by Judith Fernandez of MacMillian Publishing Co.
Noel Coward - Gertrude Lawrence from *Time*, circa 1941.
Ben D. Zevin, permission granted by Robert B. Zevin of United States Trust Co., Executor.
CBS Staffer, anonymous correspondence to the editor of *Newsday*.

XI—Musical Wit
Max Reger, from *The Best*, by Peter Passell and Leonard Ross, Farrar, Straus & Giroux Inc., approval from P. Eaton of *The New York Magazine*.
Ponselle - Pons, from *The New York Herald Tribune*, circa 1960.
Jascha Heifetz, from *This Week*, circa 1946.
Stravinsky - Rose, from *The Book of Musical Anecdotes*, The Free Press division of MacMillan, permission granted by The Free Press.

XII—Whimsical Wit
Horace Walpole, from *Converse of the Pen*, by Bruce Redford, University of Chicago Press.
Lewis Carroll, from *A Second Treasury of the World's Great Letters*, by Brockway & Winer, permission granted by Simon & Schuster.
O. Henry, letter dated July 8, 1898, from *O. Henry, A Biography*, by Smith, Doubleday Page & Co.
G. K. Chesterton, from *Ladies Home Journal*, Meredith Corp., circa 1947.
Frank N. Wilcox, letter dated June 30, 1904, permission granted by Virginia McKinnon, Westport, CT.
Arthur Train, from *My Day in Court*, Charles Scribner & Sons, Inc.
Will Rogers, from *The Will Rogers Scrapbook*, by Brian Sterling, Grosset & Dunlap.
Jackie Gleason, from the *Fort Wayne Journal Gazette*, permission granted by Larry J. Hayes, Editorial page Editor of the Ft. Wayne Journal Gazette.
Moran - Marion, letter to the editor of *The New York Times*.

XIII—Presidential Wit
Richard Nixon, letter from Sam Snead, greetings from Sam Snead but permission not specified.
Lyndon Johnson (Michener), permission granted by James Michener.
Lyndon Johnson, from *The Washington Post*, circa 1979, imaginary letter of Lyndon Johnson, permission granted by Art Buchwald.

XIV—Historic Wit

Julius Caesar, from *Ides of March,* © 1948 by Thornton Wilder. Reprinted by permission of Harper & Row.
Alexander Woolcott, from *Letters of Alexander Woolcott,* by Bernice Kaufman and Joseph Hennessy, Viking Press.

XV—Stage & Screen Wit

George S. Kaufman, from *The Saturday Review,* circa 1959.
James Thurber, from *Life* magazine.
W. S. Gilbert, from *Whatever It Is I'm Against It,* edited by Nat Shapiro, permission granted by Simon & Schuster.
Sir John Gielgud, from the *Detroit News,* permission granted by Robert Giles, Editor and Publisher of the *Detroit News.*
Cary Grant, from *Barbed Wires,* by Joyce Denebrink, permission granted by Monacle Publications.
James Stewart, from *The Letters of George Burns,* Putnam Publishing Group, permission granted by James Stewart.

XVI—TV & Radio Wit

Groucho Marx, from *Variety Magazine,* reprinted by permission of Variety Inc. "Variety" is a registered trademark of Variety Inc.
Ben Bernie - Walter Winchell, by Frederick James, from *Liberty,* circa 1931.
Garry Moore, from Bennett Cerf's column in *This Week,* circa 1959.

XVII—Tradesmen's Wit

Irvin Cobb, from *The New York Post.*
Billy Rose, from *Wine Women & Words,* by Billy Rose, Simon & Schuster.
John Steinbeck, from *Steinbeck, A Life in Letters,* by Elaine Steinbeck and Robert Wallsten, The Viking Press.
Maron Simon, correspondence to Bernard Schulist, permission granted by Maron Simon, New York, NY.
Stanley Marcus, of Neiman Marcus, Dallas, TX, permission granted by Mr. Marcus.
William Safire, from *On Language,* Doubleday Dell Publishing, permission granted by the author, William Safire.
John Yeck, from *Mottoe of the Month,* permission granted by John D. Yeck, Dayton, OH.
Beard - Collins, from *Time.*

XVIII—Clerical Wit

Kentucky Parson, from "That Reminds Me," by Alban Barkley, from *The Saturday Evening Post.*

XIX—Doctors' & Patients' Wit

Dr. Oliver Wendell Holmes, letter to the editor of *The Boston Herald.*
Dr. J.M. Mackintosh, letter dated March 6, 1933, from Trustee, The Journal for Hospital Governing Boards.
George Reedy, from "Flowers Delicious", by P. Salinger in *Reader's Digest.*
Hilarie Brown, correspondence dated March 4, 1960.
Dr. Stephen Kaufman, permission granted by Dr. Kaufman of Hastings-on-Hudson, NY.
Dr. Allen S. Johnson, correspondence to the editor of *The New England Journal of Medicine.*
Abigail VanBuren, from *The Best of Dear Abby.*
George Burns, from *Dear George,* by George Burns, Putnam Publishing Group, permission granted by Putnam Publishing Group.
Bob Hope, from *Have Tux, Will Travel.*

XX—Legal Wit

Elbert Hamlin, from *The Autobiography of William Lyon Phelps,* Oxford University Press.

XXI—Wit That is Wisdom

Albert Einstein, from *The World As I See It,* by Albert Einstein, Philosophical Library Publishers, permission granted by Philosophical Library Publishers.
H. L. Mencken, from Earl Wilson's column in *The Baltimore Sun,* permission granted by *The Baltimore Sun's* managing editor, J. Lemmon.
George Jessel, letter dated December 18, 1964, to the editor of *Time.*
Brendan Behan, letter dated 1959, Dublin, to the editor of *Time.*
Jean Cocteau, from *Inside The American College Dictionary,* circa 1959.
E.B. White, from *Letters of* E.B. White, copyright 1976 by E.B. White. Reprinted by permission of Harper & Row.
Phillip A. Davies, letter dated August 13, 1982, to the *Times* of London, from *Your Obedient Servant,* by Kenneth Gregory, Rutledge, Chapman & Hall.
Kup Kupcinet, from his column in *The Chicago Tribune.*

Index of Names